HEINEMANN
ENGLISH

David Kitchen   **Mike Hamlin**

HEINEMANN
EDUCATIONAL

Heinemann Educational,
a division of Heinemann Educational Books Ltd,
Halley Court, Jordan Hill, Oxford OX2 8EJ

OXFORD   LONDON   EDINBURGH   MADRID
ATHENS   PARIS   BOLOGNA   MELBOURNE
SYDNEY   AUCKLAND   SINGAPORE   TOKYO
IBADAN   NAIROBI   HARARE   GABORONE
PORTSMOUTH NH(USA)

First published 1991

British Library Cataloguing in Publication Data for this
title is available from the British Library.

ISBN 0 435 10304 0

Designed and illustrated by Plum Design, Southampton
Printed and bound in Great Britain, by Scotprint Ltd, Edinburgh

Introduction

Heinemann English book 3 gives you a whole range of stimulating material, including complete stories, poems, TV scripts, magazine and newspaper articles, publicity leaflets and Shakespeare.

It also has a cassette with recordings linked to the units in the book. Material on cassette is indicated in the book by a symbol like the one opposite. A full list of the cassette's contents is also given opposite.

To help you tackle the activities in the book, the reference section at the end has useful reminders about common techniques such as setting out letters and playscript. There are also photocopiable reference sheets on a large range of skills and techniques in the **Heinemann English Assessment and Reference File.**

Finally there is the **Teachers' Pack**. This provides information about classroom organisation and clear grids showing the National Curriculum coverage for each unit. The pack also contains a range of further activities and support materials.

We hope you find Heinemann English challenging and thought provoking, and, above all, enjoyable.

Cassette Contents

Contents

TRUE STORY

Not all bus journeys run smoothly. Joan Ure tells this story about one of hers.

Here is another story that isn't a joke either. Because it's true. I was travelling in the bus on the way here and the pubs had just closed when a pink-faced man got on and sat down on the first seat he could find that had a space for him. He felt in his pocket for his money, then felt in the other pocket on the other side, bumping against the Jamaican who sat at the window side of the seat. He found his fare at last, counting it out carefully, sweat standing out on his forehead from the drink. He looked at his ticket then put it in his pocket, glanced at the Jamaican and murmured, then sat with his head flopped down on his chin as if he wanted to sleep. The bus stopped with a jerk and it wakened him up. He looked around. He and the Jamaican turned to face each other. The Jamaican smiled deprecatingly and turned away to look out of the window again. He had the Guardian on his knee.

"Why don't you read your paper, man," the drunk, pink-faced man said. "Don't mind me, read your paper, man."

"Thank you," the Jamaican said in a beautiful voice, "but I've read it. Have it if you like."

"Not me," the sweating man said. "Not me, not me."

He sat for a moment longer, then as if bracing himself, and accepting a challenge, he lifted his near arm heavily from his lap and put it around the Jamaican's neck.

"We're all the same, that's what I say, we're all of us the same, no matter what the colour of our skin – black, yellow or white."

The man's face was pinker than ever and the sweat streaked brown dust along its lines. The Jamaican smiled and nodded and said nothing.

The sweating pink-faced man hung on the Jamaican's neck, falling asleep and wakening at each jerk of the bus and when he saw where he hung, he'd say again in a voice that filled the whole of the bus, "I don't hold with any of that colour bar stuff. I don't hold with it." The sweat from his forehead must have been dripping on the Jamaican's white collar, but he sat patiently, looking out of the window. At last the drunk man lifted his arm away and looked full at the Jamaican, turning sideways in his seat to do it.

"You haven't heard a word I said, have you, man?"

The Jamaican murmured, "Oh yes, oh yes," smiling rather sweetly.

The drunk man said, "No you haven't – you haven't been listening".

There was a silence and by now more people than myself were blushing at what we heard. What would happen now, we were all thinking. Then the Jamaican rose and said, "Excuse me please, this is my stop".

"What?"

"This is where I get out. This is where I live."

The whole bus waited, expecting the man to say, "You don't want to sit beside me, do you man?" But it was all right. He really was a decent man – just clumsy and a bit insensitive. He got up and called to the conductor, "Stop the bus. This gentleman wants to get off," and he pulled at the hand rail in the ceiling, remembering the old days of the string bell.

After the Jamaican had left the bus, he looked around with his fists up –

"I don't hold with any of that colour bar stuff." We were all of us quick to turn our heads away. I smiled to the Jamaican who was waiting to cross the road and at the sight of my smile, he burst out laughing. The whole bus was suddenly alight and we all began to laugh. The drunk man had fallen asleep curled up on the seat.

Reading between the lines

By looking closely at a story and discussing its content and language, you can understand more clearly what the author is saying and how she is saying it.

Divide into groups and use the following statements to help your group discuss the story.

Decide which statement in each of the following sets most accurately reflects the story in your view.

Give reasons for your decisions.

Choose a secretary to keep notes on your discussion and those decisions.

1 This kind of story is best suited to

   a) listening to as someone tells it

   b) reading in a book.

2 The Jamaican gets off the bus

   a) at the stop where he intended

   b) at an earlier stop because of the drunk.

3 The drunk

   a) isn't prejudiced

   b) is prejudiced in spite of what he says.

4 This is mainly a story

   a) about being superior

   b) about drunkenness

   c) about racial prejudice.

What did it feel like?

Once you have made your decisions, think about the attitudes and the feelings of the drunk and the Jamaican on the bus. Getting inside the characters will help you in this.

1 Agree on one person to take the part of the drunk and interview him about what happened on the bus.

2 Once you have asked the drunk about his views of the bus journey, let another person in your group take the part of the Jamaican.

3 If you have time, think and talk about uncomfortable journeys of your own. What made them awkward or unpleasant? How did they finish?

Two sides of a story

Write two short accounts of the incident: one from the drunk's point of view and one through the eyes of the Jamaican. Try to limit each account to about ten lines.

Style

Joan Ure has chosen to write in a style which often sounds like the spoken voice rather than in a more formal written style.

Read through her story and choose two sentences or phrases that you would expect to find in speech but not in more formal written English.

Try to explain your choice.

As a contrast, choose one sentence that you think is more typical of written Standard English.

> **STANDARD ENGLISH**
>
> If you are not sure what the phrase means you can find an explanation on page 148.

A different ending

Did you think the story would end in the way it did? Some people have described the ending as disappointing but others have felt it is good because it is true to life.

How else might the story end? Look over the story again up to the sentence which begins:

The whole bus waited ...

Starting from this point, write your own ending. See if you can get your own writing to sound as close to speech as the writing of Joan Ure.

EXTENSIONS

1 It is later on the same day. The Jamaican is sitting down for a quiet supper with his wife. He begins to tell her about the bus journey. What does he say?

2 It is later in the week. The drunk is now sober and is sitting in a pub with one of his friends. He begins to tell him about the bus journey. What does he say?

3 See if you can base a poem around one of the drunk's phrases. You might use it as a title, a first line or as a refrain.

The phrases you might choose include:

Don't mind me

Not me

I don't hold with any of that colour bar stuff

You haven't heard a word I said.

THE PIG'S PUDDING

Kathleen Dayus grew up in Birmingham at the turn of the century. Her family faced intense poverty, with six children and two adults having to share one living room, a bedroom and an attic; with the younger ones, Liza (11), Frankie/Francis (10) and Kathleen (8) sleeping three to a bed! But there were good times amongst the hardship, as this extract from Kathleen's autobiography shows:

All the poor children in our school were provided with a breakfast, so when the bell rang out at five minutes to nine we had to be ready and waiting. The kids from our yard would rush up the street like a lot of ants because if you were not in line when the bell stopped you would be lucky to get any at all. The breakfast consisted of an enamel mug of cocoa and two thick slices of bread and jam. The bread was usually stale or soggy. Dad would get up very early some mornings and earn himself a few extra pennies fetching the big urn which contained the cocoa, and the bread and jam. He had to wheel it along to the school in a basket carriage and when he passed our yard Mum would be waiting with a quart jug hidden underneath her apron. When she could see no one about, Dad used to fill it with cocoa. She would have helped herself to the bread and jam too but Dad stopped her because they were all counted. Mum and Dad would have been in trouble with the authorities if they'd ever been found out; but they never were. Our parents were both too cute to be caught, and although I knew what they were up to I never told anyone. I was too afraid in case they were sent to prison.

One morning we were dashing up the lane to get there in time for breakfast but the bell stopped ringing. Frankie grabbed my hand and dragged me along.

"Come on! We can still make it, Katie!" But I started to cry.

"We're too late now and I'm hungry!"

Children of the poor taken for day out to Sutton Park by the Cinderella Club, 1898

We hadn't had anything to eat since tea-time the day before, and then only a piece of bread and dripping.

"Shut yer blarting!" Liza hissed as she pushed us inside the door. Our teacher was calling the last name from the register when she saw us come in.

"I see you three are late again. I'm afraid you are too late for your breakfasts."

"But we're hungry, miss!" pleaded Frankie.

"Well you can stand at the back of the line. You may be lucky," she answered sharply.

We reached down a mug each from the ledge but when it came to our turn all we had was some warm cocoa, watered down, but no bread and jam. There was none left, and by the time our lessons were over at twelve o'clock we were very hungry.

On our way home from school we had to pass a homemade cook shop where we always paused to look through the window at all the nice things on show. This particular morning we stayed longer than usual, pressing our noses to the pane of glass, saliva dripping down our chins. There was pig's pudding, hot meat pies, hocks, tripe and cakes of every sort staring back at us. Worse than the sight of this potential feast was the smell. It was too much for Frankie who burst out: "I'm so hungry I could smash the glass in and help myself."

"And me!" I said.

"Don't you dare," said Liza, who was afraid he would.

"Well why should they be on show when we're so hungry?" asked Frankie.

Liza had no answer; she too was dribbling down her chin and she didn't stop Frankie who glanced quickly up and down the street to see who was about and hissed: "If you two look out for me and as soon as 'Skinny Legs' goes around the back of the shop I'll nip in quick and help myself to a few."

Every one called the shopkeeper this because he gave short measure and he never gave you a stale bake or a loaf like other shops did. Anyway, it seemed ages before Frankie did anything but at last he saw 'Skinny Legs' go through to the back of the shop and he dived in whilst Liza and I watched the street to warn him if anyone came along. I saw his hand in the window as he grabbed hold of a roll of pig's pudding and several hot meat pies. He came out, stuffing them under his gansey*, and the three of us ran off down the street as fast as we could but before we had gone many yards Frankie stopped.

"Catch hold of these pies, Liza, they're burning my belly!"

"No," she replied, "I don't want any part of them!"

---

* gansey: A corruption of 'guernsey', originally a fisherman's woollen jumper, but meaning here any thick, woollen sweater with a round or slit neck.

"No? But you'll take your share to eat 'em, won't you!" he snapped.

I was sure someone would come along and overhear us so I put my hands up his gansey and pulled down the pies. He wasn't kidding, they were hot, but my hands were so cold I was glad of the warmth.

"Did anyone see me?" he asked anxiously.

"Yes. He did." Liza was pointing at Jonesy, one of the lads from our yard.

"Hello, how long have you been there?" said Frankie.

"Long enough, and I seen what yer been dooin' an' all, an' if yer don't give me some I'll snitch on yer."

We all knew he meant it, so reluctantly Frankie pulled down the roll of pudding from his gansey and handed it over to Jonesy who dashed off home after saying he wouldn't tell anyone. But I knew he'd snitch all right. His mum went out cleaning on a Tuesday, so thinking she wouldn't be at home and he'd enjoy himself with his pudding he ran indoors. However he was unlucky: she was there.

"Where ever 'ave yer 'ad that from?" we heard her shout.

We heard his cringing explanation and Frankie shouted in the door, "Yer traitor."

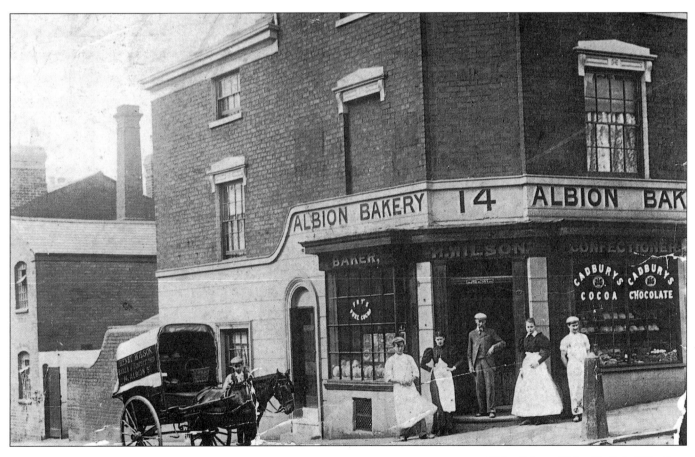

Albion Bakery, Albion St., Balsall Heath

Then the three of us ran down the yard to the washing house to eat our pies. I don't think I ever tasted anything like that meat pie. It was delicious. Afterwards as we came from the wash-house we saw Mrs Jones walking towards our house. We knew we were in trouble but we didn't care now that our appetites were satisfied. Mrs Jones didn't like our mum, in fact I don't know who did, so I wasn't surprised by what happened next. Mrs Jones knocked loudly on our door and Mum lifted the corner of the curtain to see who was there. Seeing Mrs Jones she opened wide the door and shouted for all to hear, "What do yow want?"

Mrs Jones stood on the step with her hands on her hips, grinning like a Cheshire cat. She always liked to get a dig at Mum, so she shouted louder so the neighbours could hear. "I've got news for you, Polly. Your kids 'ave pinched some of 'Skinny Legs's' pies."

She didn't mention the pig's pudding though.

"I don't believe yer and get away from my dower, the lot on yer! Goo an' look after yer own kids." And Mum slammed the door shut.

I thought, one day the door is going to fall off.

When Mrs Jones had gone away she came out again to call us in. Mrs Jones was still gossiping with the others.

"Come in, yow three. I want some explainin'."

We went in timidly, but before we could utter a word she began angrily, "An' what's this I 'ear about some pies?"

Liza quickly unburdened herself about how Frankie had stolen the pies and the pig's pudding.

"Pig's pudding. She never said anything about any pig's pudding." She was furious.

"Frankie gave it to Jonesy," said Liza.

"Well, we'll see about that!" said Mum.

She was fuming. She couldn't get out of the house quick enough. On went Dad's cap, off came the apron, and round the backyard she marched. When she got to Mrs Jones's door she banged twice, as hard as she could. All of the neighbours lifted their windows and popped their heads out while some of them crowded round to watch developments more closely. They knew Mum was big enough to eat Mrs Jones. There was no answer so she knocked again, louder and shouted, "Yow can come out. I've seen yer be'ind the curtin."

Slowly, Mrs Jones opened the door a little way to face

No.6 Court, Essington St. This is similar to the house in which Kathleen Dayus grew up.

Mum standing there, hands on hips, chest puffed out.

"Yer crafty old sod! Yow never told me that my Frankie giv' your lad a roll of pig's pudding. Now what about it? An' I ain't gooin' from 'ere till I get it."

Mrs Jones was scared now, thinking what Mum might do, so she shut the door quickly and we all heard the bolt rammed home. But Mum wasn't finished. She banged again, louder than ever.

"Yer better 'and over that puddin' or else!" demanded Mum, her fist in the air. Then suddenly the window shot up and the pig's pudding come flying out. It caught Mum on the head and everyone began laughing, but Mum ignored them and grabbed hold of us and the pudding and marched us indoors. She never bothered about what the neighbours thought or said as long as she didn't hear them. Woe betide them if she did.

Courtyard, Cromwell St., 1904. This is similar to the one in which Kathleen Dayus lived.

"Get yer clo's off and get up them stairs. I'll get yer dad ter deal with you two when 'e comes 'ome."

She pushed us towards the stairs and Frankie and I ran quickly up to the attic. We didn't go back to school that afternoon because Mum kept us up there until Dad returned in the evening and all we had to eat that day was the meat pie each.

It was late when we heard Dad come up the stairs so we pretended to be asleep. We knew he wouldn't wake us. Sure enough we soon heard his receding footsteps on the stairs. In the early hours of the morning Frankie crept downstairs and brought a cup of water and a thick slice of bread and lard. We shared this between us while Liza slept on. Then we climbed back into bed and finally fell asleep.

Getting to know you

Six characters are described in this extract. Select two quotations from the account which tell you something about each of these characters. For example, the very first thing which Liza "hisses" to Kathleen is "Shut yer blarting!" as she "pushed us inside the door" – this clearly tells us something of the nature of Liza.

Write these quotations on a sheet of paper.

When you have finished, compare your selections with those of another member of your group. See if together you can agree on a final six quotes which best capture the characters described.

Fact or fiction?

This extract claims to be from an autobiography but it reads as if it could have been taken from a fictional story.

Read through the piece again, listing all the things which convince you that this is a truthful account of someone's life rather than a work of imagined fiction. For example, look carefully at the way breakfast is described, the detail of the enamel mug of cocoa, the two thick slices of bread and jam with the bread tending to be stale or soggy. Surely such detail suggests a real rather than an imagined experience?

What other things help to create this sense of realism?

Could they just be the tricks of a clever writer?

 The interview with Kathleen Dayus on the accompanying cassette will help you with all of these activities.

Speaking for real

Now look carefully at the way the characters in the passage speak to each other. There is an attempt to show the way they pronounce certain words; their accent. Unusual words and phrases are also used to show that a regional dialect is being spoken.

For example, instead of saying "stop your crying" Liza says "shut yer blarting". When Frankie stuffs the roll of pig's pudding "under his gansey", Jonesy reminds him that "I seen what yer been dooin' an' all, an' if yer don't give me some I'll snitch on yer.".

This mixture of accent – your pronounced as yer, dooin' instead of doing, and dialect words such as blarting, gansey and snitch – make the piece sound real as well as injecting some life and vitality.

In pairs, read through the rest of the extract again. As you go, one person writes down whenever accent is used, the other records each example of dialect. In this way you will be able to see just how much care the writer has taken to capture the way the characters speak to each other.

Over the garden fence

Write the conversation that neighbours, perhaps the Joneses, might have when describing the Dayus family and their exploits. Think carefully about the way your characters would speak, especially their accents and any dialect words they might use.

My story

Make a collection of your own autobiographical fragments. You could start by using some of the themes suggested by Kathleen Dayus, later adding ideas of your own:

I was so hungry I could ...

Snitching on a friend

Getting your own back

Sticking up for a brother or sister

What must the neighbours think?

Don't do as I do, do as I say!

Life is just not fair ...

Test out a variety of approaches – memories, poems, descriptive pieces – but try to keep a reader's interest by using a lively, entertaining style.

Growing up today

The scenes described by Kathleen Dayus occurred over eighty years ago.

In what ways is growing up today different from the past?

What new pressures are faced by today's young people?

For example, when Frankie took the pig's pudding from the butchers, he was really stealing it and therefore guilty of shoplifting. Today such a crime would be likely to land him in front of the magistrates!

Have attitudes towards theft changed over the years, or have some types of theft always been more acceptable than others?

Does this mean that growing up is easier or more difficult today?

Talk these issues through in small groups before writing up your own ideas.

FLAT TYRE

Writing a story

a

As you have seen in the first two units, one of the most important parts of a story is its characters. Another is its plot - what happens during the story.

See if you can create a plot for a story which involves the first three pictures here, **a,b** and **c**, and one of the two final pictures, **d** or **e**.

You are free to imagine that the pictures are in any order you wish so long as the story is convincing and believable.

You might call your story **Flat Tyre** or you may prefer to use a title of your own.

b

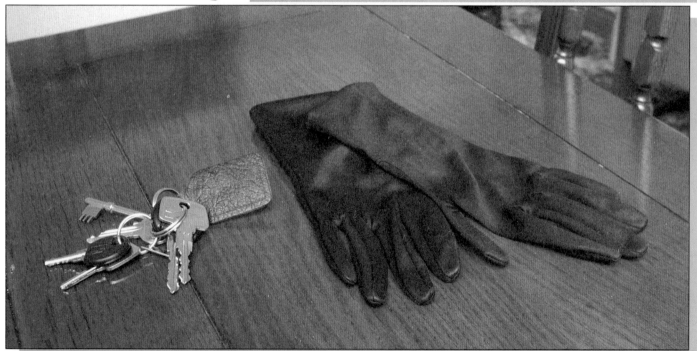

c

d

e

In pairs

Your work can often be improved by discussing it with other people.

There are two moments in this activity when it might be helpful to find out what another person thinks of your ideas:

- when you have made your original plans
- when you have written the first draft of your story.

MISTER
MUSHROOMS

This is one of those stories in which you soon start to wonder what is going to happen. Keep a piece of rough paper by you and whenever you think you know what is about to occur, write it down briefly. If you change your mind, add a few more notes to remind you of how your thinking altered.

The war was a bad thing of course, but Kenneth Dunn couldn't help hoping it might last a few years yet. He wanted to get into it and be a hero, like his dad in the last one. He was fed up of the other kids making fun of him. They made fun of him because of his mum, his liberty-bodice and Mister Mushrooms.

Kenneth's mum fussed too much. She was always frightened he might catch cold or chicken-pox or double-pneumonia. She made him eat his greens and dosed him daily with cod-liver oil. She had him in shoes when everybody else was in sandals and in gumboots when the others wore shoes. If he went out to play, she'd warn him not to play with certain children, and not to go too far. And all the time he was out she'd hover by the parlour window, standing on tiptoe to see him over the privet hedge.

He knew why she was like that. It was because he was her only child and because his dad was dead. The trouble was, the others didn't understand. They called him a mammy's boy, and when they changed for P.T. at school they'd nudge one another and snigger because he was wearing a liberty-bodice. A liberty-bodice was a horrible fleecy white thing with no sleeves, which you wore between your vest and your shirt. It could be worn by boys or girls and had stupid tapes dangling down so girls could fasten it to their knickers. It kept you warm but it was sissy, and Kenneth was the only boy in his class who wore one.

And then there was Mister Mushrooms. His real name was Mr Smith and he was the lodger. For some reason, the kids found the idea of a lodger highly amusing, though Kenneth couldn't for the life of him see why. Mr Smith was simply a paying guest who lived in his mother's spare room; a short, rather plump little man with wire-rimmed glasses and a cropped moustache. His job, which he couldn't talk about because it had something to do with the war, took him away a lot. He'd be gone, two, three, sometimes four days at a stretch. When he wasn't away he'd keep to his room, coming down only at mealtimes, or potter about for hours in the garden shed. The shed had belonged to Kenneth's dad and had fallen into disuse at his death so, when Mr Smith had asked if he might make use of it, Mrs Dunn had said yes. Mr Smith had then bought a padlock for it without asking, which Kenneth thought a bit of a cheek, and now nobody except Mr Smith could get in.

Once, while he was away on one of his trips, Kenneth had tried to look through the window of the shed, but Mr Smith had fastened a piece of cardboard over it on the inside. This made Kenneth really mad, and when the man returned a day or two later he asked him, straight out, what he was doing in there. Mr Smith told him that he was growing mushrooms.

"Mushrooms?" Kenneth exclaimed. "Wizard! Shall we be having some for tea, Mr Smith?" Wartime meals were boring, and Kenneth loved mushrooms.

"No," replied Mr Smith, disdainfully. "Certainly not. I am not growing that kind of mushroom. I am growing special mushrooms: tropical ones, and they are deadly poisonous, which is why I am always locking the shed."

"But if the mushrooms are poisonous," said Kenneth, "what's the point of growing them?"

"It's a hobby," Mr Smith told him. "I am a mycologist."

When he mentioned the matter to his mother she said, "Well, I don't know why anybody would want to grow poisonous mushrooms in a garden shed but that's Mr Smith's business. You are to keep away from them; right away, d'you hear?"

"Yes, Mum," he sighed, and went off to tell his two chums Bill and Ernest who, as soon as they heard the story, christened the lodger "Mister Mushrooms". The nickname made the little man seem even funnier, and the ragging intensified till he wished he'd kept his mouth shut.

A few weeks later, though, something happened which drove Mister Mushrooms clear out of everybody's mind. A chilling rumour went round that the enemy had developed a secret weapon. This weapon, the rumour said, was a bombsight: a fiendish instrument which enabled German bomb-aimers to see their targets on the ground, even in total darkness. The blackout, in which everybody covered their windows before switching on a light, was useless now. The enemy fliers didn't need lights to show them where their targets were. England, said the rumour, was a sitting duck.

Nobody really knew how the rumour started. Somebody's dad knew somebody who had been in Manchester on a moonless night when enemy planes scored twenty direct hits on a blacked-out factory. Somebody else heard that warehouses in London had been wiped out in the same way; the bombs falling with uncanny accuracy, and a couple of fellows thought they'd heard soldiers talking in a train about a tank-repair shop, blasted out of existence though it lay camouflaged in the midst of fields.

There had been rumours before: there always are in wartime. Rumours of enemy submarines in the Thames, parachutists on the downs and jack-booted invaders on the Isle of Wight. Most of these stories were so far-fetched that they died out almost at once, while others were killed off by denials from the BBC. This one hung around, growing stronger as stories continued to flow in of vital installations obliterated with pinpoint accuracy. Some of the stories began appearing in newspapers. No denials came over the wireless, and within a short time it became obvious to everyone that the secret weapon was a fact.

"Isn't it awful?" said Mrs Dunn one teatime. A newspaper lay folded beside her plate. "It feels like last year, when we were expecting an invasion and everybody was on edge. I don't like it at all."

Kenneth put down his fork and curled his hand into a fist. "I wish I was eighteen," he growled. "I'd be a Spitfire pilot and they wouldn't get near enough to use their rotten bombsight." Nobody'd laugh at me then, he added silently.

"Well I'm glad you're not eighteen," said his mother. "One hero in a family's enough: coming home all shot up and dying before his time." She was thinking about her husband of course.

Mister Mushrooms, toying with his beans on toast, said, "I shouldn't worry, Mrs Dunn. They'll find a way of beating this bombsight." He gave a little laugh, adding, "If it is a bombsight." Kenneth looked at him. "Course it's a bombsight," he said, rudely.

"Kenneth!" His mother looked shocked.

"Well," mumbled Kenneth, looking at his plate. "What else could it be?"

Mister Mushrooms dabbed at his faintly smiling lips, folded his napkin and rose. "Strange things happen in wartime," he murmured. "Strange inventions; funny going-ons. One can never tell. And now if you'll excuse me I'll go to my room."

When he'd gone, Mrs Dunn spoke sternly to her son. "That was extremely rude of you, Kenneth," she reproved. "You're to go upstairs at once, knock on Mr Smith's door and apologise." Kenneth nodded glumly. "All right, Mum. But there's something about him I don't like. All the boys call him Mister Mushrooms, you know." He got up and left the room.

The lodger was a long time answering his knock. When the door opened, Kenneth saw a suitcase open on the bed and papers on the table. Mister Mushrooms looked irritated at the disturbance. "Yes?"

Kenneth looked down, shuffling his feet. "Mum says I was rude to you. I'm sorry."

"That's all right," said the lodger, coldly. "Boys are often rude. Tell your mother I wish breakfast at seven tomorrow: I must catch the eight-fifteen to Birmingham and will be away till Thursday."

Next morning, when Mister Mushrooms had gone, Kenneth went down to the shed again. He rattled the door, peered at the covered window and walked round the back in the hope of finding a knot-hole or crack. There was nothing.

"I'll have a dekko in there if it's the last thing I do," he muttered to himself. "I'll do it tonight, after school." He didn't know why he wanted to look in the shed, except that Mister Mushrooms obviously didn't want him to.

That evening, Kenneth spent a long time outside the back door, cleaning his bike. It was September, and it didn't get dark till late. It would have to be dark when he tackled the shed, because his mother had told him to keep away from it. At half-past nine he stuck his head round the door. It was dusk.

"I'm off for a spin, Mum," he called. "I've adjusted the brakes and I want to test them."

"Very well, dear," his mother replied. "Keep off the main road and don't be long: it's almost dark and motorists can't see you in the blackout."

He did go for a spin, but only down the pathway to the shed. He wheeled the bike round the back, propped it against the wall and opened his saddle-bag. Inside was a puncture-outfit and a jumble of tools. He selected a slim tyre-lever, slipped round the side of the shed and looked towards the house. His mother had drawn thick curtains over all the windows. No chink of light fell on pathway or lawn. He moved silently to the door of the shed and set to work.

He knew that what he was doing was wrong. He'd lied to his mother and now he was forcing a lock. If he'd thought for a moment he'd never have done it but something had taken hold of him; some force that drove him on, overriding his timid nature. He felt bold and strong and excited, and wondered momentarily if this was how his father had felt all those years ago, charging alone over shell-torn mud towards the enemy machine-gun; for he had been a gentle person too. And he felt something else; a conviction that what he was doing was vital: the chance he'd prayed for to play a part in the war. It was crazy, but it drove him on.

The lock snapped open. With fumbling fingers he tore it from the hasp. The door swung inwards and he gasped, screwing up his eyes. The shed was indeed full of mushrooms. Trayful after trayful, and every mushroom glowed with a cold green luminescence. He stood for a moment, gazing at the strange fungi. Then he pulled the door to, hooked the broken padlock in the hasp and hurried round the back to fetch his bike.

He said nothing to his mother but lay tense in his bed that night, till he heard her go to hers. A half-hour more he waited, then slipped from his room and crossed the landing with a flashlight in his hand.

The lodger's door was locked. His mother kept a key so that she could clean. He crept down the creaky stairs and found it. Ascending swiftly, he let himself in, closed the door and stood with his back to it, playing the torch beam slowly across the room. A faint smell like scent hung on the air. A pair of carpet slippers lay by the hearth and there were cufflinks and collar-studs on the dressing table.

He crossed the room and began going through the drawers, his scalp tingling. Pulling them open one by one, he shone the torch in and flipped through the contents. Socks, underwear, handkerchiefs. Little jars and bottles. Razor blades and a pair of braces. He moved to the wardrobe. An overcoat hung between some trousers and a suit. There were ties behind the door and three pairs of shoes on the floor. A green glass ashtray stood on the mantel and the hearth was clean.

Kenneth stood in the middle of the room. He didn't know what he'd hoped to find. Documents, perhaps. Detectives in books always found documents, unless the villain had been warned, in which case they found ashes of burnt paper in the grate. Maybe he's not a villain at all, he thought, gloomily. Maybe I've been kidding myself. As a last resort, he got down on his knees and shone the torch under the bed. In the depression made by a castor in the carpet lay a scrap of paper. Kenneth plucked it out and shone the torch on it.

It was a torn fragment, hardly bigger than his thumbnail, but there was something written on it in pencil. His lips moved slightly as he tried to decipher the pale script.

"am am 7 Okt. brennt." Am. The first two letters had probably been part of a longer word because they were on a torn edge, but then there was another "am." Am am 7 Okt. brennt. Something ending in am, then am, then a funny seven followed by Okt., and brennt. With a pounding heart, he realised that the words were in a foreign language. Mister Mushrooms, who called himself Smith, was a foreigner. Could he be a German?

Kenneth locked the door, returned the key to its place and took the scrap of paper to his room. He sat with the dim night-light on, staring at the pencilled words. 7 Okt. Could be the seventh of October. That was in two weeks' time. Maybe something important was to happen on that date, but what? If only he could understand the rest, it might tell him.

Suddenly an idea occurred to him. There was a teacher at school, Mr Vale, who taught languages. Latin, French and German. If these words were in German ----. He nodded and smiled. That was the next step: Mr Vale. He put the scrap of paper in his bedside drawer and lay down. His heart was pounding, and sleep was a long time coming.

He couldn't show Mr Vale the fragment of course, so he copied the word "brennt" into his jotter and caught the master in the corridor at breaktime. "Excuse me, sir?"

"What is it, lad?" Mr Vale wanted his cup of tea. Kenneth held out the jotter. "Is this a German word please, sir?"

Mr Vale peered at it. "Brennt," he said. "Yes, lad; it means 'burns'." Kenneth's heart gave a lurch.

"Burns, sir?"

"Burns," confirmed Mr Vale. "Why d'you ask?"

"Oh, it's nothing really sir," said Kenneth. "A chum told me it was German and I bet him it wasn't."

"Then you lost," said the teacher with a tight smile. "So off you go and pay up like a good chap while I have my tea."

Kenneth grinned ruefully. "Yes, sir, thank you sir." The teacher was turning away when, on an impulse, Kenneth added, "What about 'am' sir?"

"On." Mr Vale flung the word over his shoulder. "On, to weak, sugarless tea and no biscuit."

Kenneth grinned at the retreating back. Everybody hated rationing: even Mr Vale.

After school, Kenneth called at a hardware shop and bought a padlock like the one he had forced the night before. It was a cheap type and he was almost certain it had the same keys as the old one. He swapped the locks and pocketed the keys. The old one had spots of rust on it, but so would the new one after a day or two. He was fairly sure Mister Mushrooms wouldn't spot the changeover.

After tea he went to his room with his jotter and the scrap of paper. He wrote, "- am on the seventh of October burns," and sat gazing at the words. Something burns on the seventh of October; something ending in "am." Spam perhaps, or jam. Or Pam, that good-looking girl in the lower sixth. It wasn't funny, really. He chewed his lip in frustration, wondering whether he ought to tell somebody.

Ham. He got a mental picture of ham sizzling in a pan, with two eggs. His mouth filled with water and his stomach yearned. His mind leap-frogged and he jumped up with a cry. Ham. Burning ham. Birmingham! "Birmingham on the seventh of October burns." Now he knew he was onto something, but what?

He began pacing the room, hands in pockets, muttering to himself. Birmingham. Mister Mushrooms was in Birmingham. Birmingham on the seventh of October burns. How? He knew he ought to go to the police, but what evidence had he? A scrap of paper and a shedful of luminous mushrooms. Why would a German spy grow fungus in a shed? It was daft, and yet ----.

Something stirred at the back of his mind. Luminous mushrooms. Moominous lushrooms. He went to the window and stood looking down into the garden. The shed was faintly visible in the twilight. Luminous mushrooms. That was why the man had put cardboard over the window: not to stop people seeing in, but so that the eerie glow wouldn't escape and spoil the blackout.

The blackout. He stared down at the shed. Something stirred again, quickening. The shed. The blackout. If there was no cardboard over that window, then from up here, from up there... That was it! It must be. It was fantastic and impossible but it had to be the truth. Trembling, he turned from the window, grabbed jotter and pencil and sat on the edge of the bed. Keep calm. He must keep calm: think it through and be sure.

Biology class last year. Moulds and fungi: reproduction by spores. Mushrooms spawn in your drawers. Spawn. Suppose you take spawn from a luminous mushroom. Suppose you scatter it on the ground near – an aircraft factory, for example. Then, when the mushrooms come up, they glow, and ----.

No. He frowned, rapping the jotter with his pencil. No good. Somebody'd spot them. Then how? Where? It had to be right: it had to be. Got it! So obvious was the answer that he leaped up and spoke aloud.

"On top. He scatters it on top of buildings; on roofs. There's dirt there, on ledges and sills and things. Pigeon-dirt. Soot. That's it!"

The secret weapon: the bombsight. It wasn't a bombsight at all, it was a mushroom: a luminous mushroom and he'd cracked the mystery: he, Kenneth Dunn in his liberty-bodice. The kid with the fussy mum. He was sure now: dead sure. He had only to telephone the police and he'd be a hero. "If it is a bombsight," Mister Mushrooms had said. "Going ons," instead of "Goings-on." "I am growing special mushrooms." Everything fitted.

He was at the door with his hand on the knob when he heard voices downstairs. His mother's and another: a man's voice, raised in agitation. The voice of Mister Mushrooms. Kenneth went cold. He'd said Thursday and it was only Wednesday. He sounded angry. And this wasn't Mister Mushrooms the odd lodger: it was Herr somebody-or-other, the ruthless German spy!

A door opened. The man's voice came more loudly. He was in the hall. "That's what I said!" he cried. "Tampered with. Changed. That very rude boy of yours I expect: anyway I'm leaving, now: tonight!" Footsteps on the stairs and his mother's voice pleading.

"Mr Smith, please. It's dark out there; how can you be sure ...?"

Kenneth saw the man's shadow under his door, felt his angry footfalls. A door slammed, and he heard sounds of hurried movement: drawers being flung open in the lodger's room. His mother was coming up the stairs. What to do? The man was packing. He'd spotted the new lock and knew the game was up. A couple of minutes and he'd be gone: slipping away into the darkness to start up somewhere else. He must act, quickly, like Dad.

In a drawer in his mother's room was the German pistol his dad had brought back as a souvenir. It was empty, but the man wouldn't know that. Suppose...? He groaned, hitting his forehead with the heel of his hand. Suppose what? Suppose he got the pistol, intercepted the man on the landing and said, "Hands up." What would happen? His mother would think he'd gone mad. She'd scream or faint or something, instead of calling the police. Mister Mushrooms would laugh at him and start down the stairs, and he'd be left like a fool with his empty gun.

He was picturing this scene when he heard the lodger's door open and his mother said, "Mr Smith –". Rapid footfalls, heading for the stairs. With the courage of desperation, Kenneth wrenched open the door and came out onto the landing. His mother was at the top of the stairs and Mister Mushrooms, suitcase in hand, was passing her on the way down.

"Stop!" The man glanced round and Kenneth yelled, "Mum' he's a German. I've got proof!" It happened just as he had known it would. His mother's jaw dropped and she gave him the sort of look she might give as they dragged him off to the loony-bin. Mister Mushrooms laughed. "Mrs Dunn, your son is mad, I think." He passed on down the stairs.

"Mum!"
Kenneth ran to
her, grabbed her by the
shoulders. "I found a
message, in German, in his room.
The shed's full of luminous mushrooms.
Help me, Mum!"

"Kenneth!" She loosed his grip and tried to take him in
her arms. The front door slammed. He twisted, breaking free.
"I'm all right, Mum, really!" He looked beyond her. "Oh, God, I must
do something; he's getting away!" His mother reached for him, her face
creased with concern. He dodged and plunged past her, down the stairs.

Outside it was dark and cool. The front gate stood open. Kenneth ran
down the path and glanced both ways. The lampless road was thick with
shadows that seemed to move. As he hesitated, almost sobbing with
frustration, there came a faint low moaning sound which swelled and rose,
then dipped and rose again.

The siren! His scalp prickled. From within the house his mother's vioce
screamed, "Kenneth!" He turned left and began running in the direction of
the railway station. He'd gone less than fifty yards when a dark figure
loomed before him and he felt himself grabbed. He kicked and struggled,
his gasps drowned by the siren. Strong arms tightened round him and a
gruff voice in his ear said, "Steady lad, steady: we'll find you a shelter in a
jiffy."

"I don't want a shelter!" He'd recognised the voice of the local bobby. "Let
go, Mr Collins, please: there's a spy and he's getting away!"

"Spy?" The policeman's grip slackened. "What're you on about, son?
There's no spy here, but Gerry'll be over any minute so let's get under
cover, eh?"

"There is a spy!" He was crying now, but he didn't care. He had to make the man believe him. "He was staying with us. I found some proof and he ran. Let me show you, Mr Collins, please!" The constable bit his lip and glanced at the sky. It all sounded a bit unlikely to him but the kid was obviously upset. And him usually such a sensible kid too. He made his decision. "All right, lad; show me. Only make it snappy, see?"

Kenneth turned, running back the way he had come. The policeman followed. They passed his mother by the gate.

"Kenneth!" she cried.

"Get under cover, Missus!" yelled the constable.

Kenneth led him along the side of the house and across the lawn to the shed. The siren was dying and the sound of engines swelled to fill the sky.

"Hurry up, lad!" cried the policeman. "Where's this proof of yours?"

"Here!" The lock hung loose. Kenneth tore it out, flung it aside and threw back the door of the shed.

The policeman flung up his hands to shield his eyes as green luminescence flooded the night. From high in the sky overhead the roar reached a crescendo and a voice out of the blackness cried, "Put that light out!"

Robert Swindells

Predictions

Did the the story work out as you thought it would?

Did your ideas about what was going to happen change as the story developed?

If you found that you couldn't predict the story, what effect did this have on your reading of it?

How did you feel about the ending?

What do you think would have happened next if the story had continued?

Looking at the detail

1 What do you discover about Kenneth's family?

2 In what ways is life different because of the war?

3 What words or phrases in the story give you a sense of it being over fifty years ago rather than today?

Is he a spy?

Kenneth is in no doubt by the end of the story that Mr Smith is a spy.

What is the evidence? In your groups, discuss the case for and the case against the accusation that Kenneth makes to Constable Collins.

1 What proof is there that Mr Smith has been spying?

2 What are the weaknesses in the case?

In the Hot Seat

If Mr Smith turns out to be a spy, what do you think each of the following would have to say about what happened:

Kenneth

Mrs Dunn

Constable Collins?

1 Take it in turns to each play the part of one of the characters whilst the others ask you questions about what your character thought and did.

2 Now imagine that Mr Smith turns out not to have been spying at all. What would the characters say in that situation?

Kenneth, Bill and Ernest

What do you think Kenneth and his two friends would have to say to each other in the school yard on the day after this incident if:

1 Mr Smith has disappeared and nothing has been sorted out

2 Mr Smith has been caught and charged with spying

3 Mr Smith has explained himself and has been seen not to be a spy?

Choose one of these possibilities and write a short scene which might have happened.

PLAYSCRIPT

If you need help with playscript or the layout of conversation, look at pages 156 and 154.

An alternative ending: my choice

Write the next page or two of this story to end it in the way that you think best.

The choice is up to you but you might like to think about:

- what happens that night
- how Constable Collins follows up what has happened
- the mushrooms in the shed
- the air raids.

A POTTLE O' BRAINS

An old tale from Lincolnshire in England

Once in these parts, and not so long ago, there lived a wise old dame. Some said she was a fairy, but they said it in a whisper, in case she should overhear and do them mischief.

If you were ill, she could tell you how to cure yourself with herbs; and she could mix possets that would drive out pain in a twinkling. She could advise you what to do if your cows took sick or if you had toothache; and she could tell the lads and lasses if their sweethearts were untrue.

One day, as she sat at her door peeling potatoes, over the stile and up the path came a tall lad with big ears and goggle eyes, hands in pockets.

"That's a fool, if ever was," said the wise old dame, nodding her head. And she threw some potato peel over her left shoulder for luck.

"Evenin', missis," says he, "tis a fine night for it."

"Aye," says she, and went on peeling.

"It'll maybe rain," says he, shifting from right foot to left.

"Maybe," says she.

"And maybe it won't," says he, looking at the sky.

"Maybe not," says she.

He took off his hat and scratched his head.

"Well," says he, "that's the weather done, now let me see ... The crops are doing fine."

"Fine," says she.

"And the pigs are fattening," says he.

"They are that," says she.

"And, and ..." says he, coming to a halt. "I reckon I'll get down to business now: have you any brains to sell?"

"That depends," says she. "If you want king's brains, priest's brains, judge's brains, I don't stock them."

"Oh no," says he, "just ordinary pottle o'brains, same as folk about here have, something common-like."

"Well, then," says the woman, "I might manage that if you can help yourself."

"How's that, missus?" says he.

"Just so," says she, eyeing her potatoes. "Bring me the heart of the thing you like the best, and I'll tell you where to get your brains." He scratched his head. "How can I do that?" he says.

"That's not for me to say," says she. "Find out for yourself, lad, unless you wish to be stupid all your days. And you must also answer me a riddle, so I can see you have your wits about you. Now, good evening." And she took her pile of potatoes indoors.

So off went the fool to his mother and told her of the wise woman's words.

"I reckon I'll have to kill our pig," says he, "for I like pork scratchings best of all."

"Then do it, lad," his mother says. "For certain, 'twill be a good thing for you if you can look after yourself."

So he kills his pig, and next day goes off to the wise woman's place. And there she sat, reading a great book.

"Evenin', missis," says he, "I've brought you the heart of the thing I like the best. I'll leave it on the table all wrapped up."

"Aye so," says she, peering at him over her spectacles. "Here's your riddle then: What runs without feet?"

He took off his hat and scratched his head; he thought and thought but could not tell.

"Go on your way," says she, "for you've not brought the right thing yet. I've no brains for you today."

With that she clapped the book together and turned her back. So he went back down the path and over the stile and sat down by the roadside to cry. And how he cried. By and by, up came a lass who lived nearby.

"What's up, lad? Can I help?"

"Oooo, I've killed my pig, but cannot gain a pottle o'brains," wails he.

"What are you talking about?"

And down she sits beside him to hear about the wise woman and the pig. He says, besides, he has no one to look after him.

"Well," says she, "I wouldn't mind living with you myself."

"Could you do it?" says he, surprised.

"Oh, I dare say," says she. "Folk say that fools make decent husbands. I reckon I might have you. Can you cook?"

"Aye, I can," says he.

"And scrub?"

"Surely."

"And mend my clouts?"

"I can that," says he.

"Then I reckon you'll do as well as anybody," says she.

"That's settled then," says he. "I'll come and fetch you when I've told my Ma."

He gave her his lucky penny and went off home.

When he got home and told his mother he wished to marry, the poor woman was very cross.

"What!" says she. "*That* lass? No, and that you'll not. She does men's work in the fields and never keeps a clean and tidy house. And there's talk about her in the neighbourhood."

"But I gave her my lucky penny," he says.

"Then you're a bigger fool than ever," says his mother.

Those were the last words the poor woman spoke. For she was so upset that she lay right down and died.

So down sat the fool and the more he thought about it the worse he felt. He remembered how she had nursed him when he was a little lad, and helped him with his sums; and how she had cooked his dinners, and mended his shirts, and put up with his foolish ways; and he felt sorrier and sorrier and began to sob.

"Oh, Ma, Ma," wails he, "I liked you best of all."

As he said that, he thought of the wise dame's words.

"Hout-tout!" says he. "Must I take her my Ma's heart?"

He thought and thought and scratched his head; then an idea came to him. He took a sack and pushed his mother in. Then he hoisted her on his shoulder and carried her up to the old dame's place.

"Evenin', missis," says he. "I reckon I've fetched the right thing this time." And he plumped the sack down upon the table.

"Maybe," says she. "But tell me this: What's yellow and shining, yet isn't gold?"

He scratched his head, but could not tell.

"You've not found the right thing yet, my lad," says she. "You're a bigger fool than I thought." And she shut the door, bang, right in his face.

Feeling sad, off he went to the lass he had met and got himself married to her. He kept the house clean and neat, and cooked her fine dinners; and she worked hard in the fields all day. It pleased them both.

One night he says to her, "Lass, I'm thinking I like you best of all."

"That's good to hear," says she. "And what then?"

"Should I kill you, do you think, and take your heart up to the wise dame for that pottle o'brains?"

"Lawks, no!" says she, getting scared. "See here, just you take me to her as I am, heart and all, and I'll help you solve those riddles."

"Will you so?" says he, doubtful-like. "I reckon they're too hard for womenfolk."

"Well," says she, "just test me now."

"What runs without feet?" says he.

"Why, water, of course!" says she.

"Aye, so it does," says he, scratching his head.

"And what's yellow and shining, yet isn't gold?" says he.

"Why, the sun, of course!" says she.

"Faith, so it is," says he. "Come, we'll go to the dame at once."

And off they went. As they came up the path and over the stile, she was sitting at the door, twining straws.

"Evenin', missis," says he.

"Evenin', Fool," says she.

"I reckon I've fetched you the right thing at last."

The wise woman looked at them both and wiped her spectacles.

"Answer my riddles then," she says. "What has first no legs, then two legs, then four legs?"

The fool scratched his head, thought and thought, but could not tell.

So the lass whispered in his ear, "A tadpole".

"Happen it's a tadpole, missis," says he at last.

The old dame nodded. "Now what about the other riddles?"

At once he told her what his wife had said: water and the sun.

The wise woman smiled. "You've got your pottle o'brains at last," says she.

"Where are they?" says he, looking about and feeling his head.

"In your wife's head," says she. "The only cure for a fool is a good wife. Good evenin' to you!"

The fool and his wife walked home together, quite content. And he never wished for brains again, for his wife had enough for two.

Group work

After reading **A Pottle o'Brains**, work in groups of four – a wise woman, a foolish lad, his mother, a clever lass – and improvise the main parts of the story again.

By improvising it through you will be making more sense of the story and its message.

Put to the test

This story, like many other folk tales, revolves around a series of "tests" which the main character has to attempt in order to achieve something.

Still in small groups, talk through a number of other stories which work in this way. For example, some tales use a test of having to find something – a one-eyed fish perhaps! Others make a character do something unusual, like remain totally silent for three years or stay awake throughout the telling of the world's most boring story.

Talk through as many as you can remember; you might like to improvise some of them as well.

That's different

A Pottle o'Brains ends with the lad and the lass getting married – " He kept the house clean and neat, and cooked her fine dinners; and she worked hard in the fields all day. It pleased them both."

Is this a typical way for stories like this to end?

What else is different in this particular story, compared with others you have read or heard?

Write down as many examples as you can find, explaining why they are different.

A game of stories

Traditional stories like **A Pottle o'Brains** could easily be represented by a series of diagrams or picture cards. For instance, the cards would certainly need to contain a heroine or a hero, an evil one, a wise person, a joker and a fool. Other cards would need to show a range of tests and trials, wrong roads would sometimes be taken as the search progresses. Providing all goes well, wisdom and happiness would at last be found as the quest is successfully completed. However, should things go wrong ... a range of horrible fates lies waiting!

Your teacher will give you a pack of story cards. Arrange or display them in a connected sequence to make the most exciting range of story possibilities. You can change the characters as you wish, to make them science fiction or traditional fairy tale, male or female, but you must keep their roles in the story the same.

A Wise Woman

"Unless you wish to be stupid all your days ... you must think things out for yourself."

This was the advice of the wise woman early on in the story and it remained true at the end. Stay with this idea and invent your own "wise woman" story.

Aim it at readers your own age but as with **A Pottle o'Brains** try to turn tradition on its head! You may prefer to write a modern day version – fine, it will need a new title and the characters and setting will change, but try to keep the central idea the same.

Possible titles are:

Winnie the wise

Three strong women

The case of the nagging husband

but there are many others.

Above all – have fun.

HOW DID IT GET THERE ?

Group work

Choose one of the pictures and come up with as many explanations of it as you can.

Write them all down.

When you run out of ideas, decide on the best three or four and add any further details you can come up with as a group.

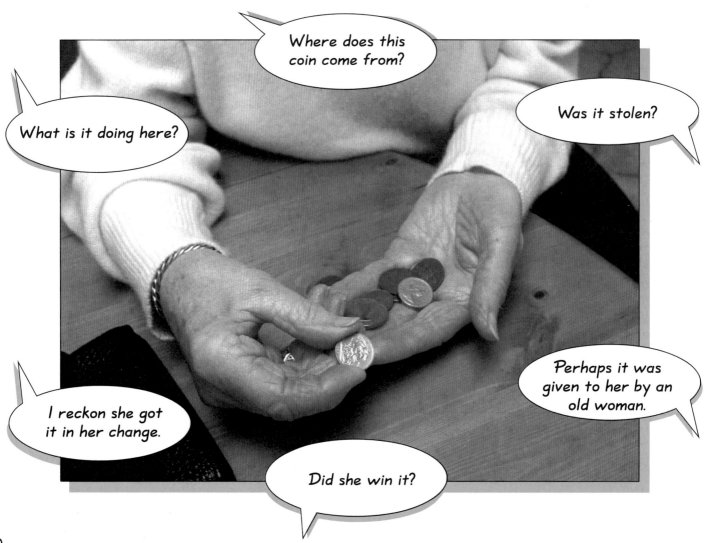

Individual work

Choose one of the ideas you developed and use it as the basis for a piece of writing. (This might be a diary/story/ newspaper article.)

Further work

You may wish to get together as a group and share what you have written.

In what ways might the stories you wrote be improved?

What works well in them?

I AM LARGE, I CONTAIN MULTITUDES

**"It's not only that I'm afraid of being broken –
though I am. But if I break, who will take care
of my multitudes? Who will feed and clothe
them? I have to protect myself, for their sake."**

As you are reading think about:

- what you think is happening
- what you think is going wrong
- what you think might happen at the end

I am large, I contain multitudes. They speak to me
from time to time. I never answer. I am too busy.
Even when they shout and plead. I can't take time for
them. I've more important things to do.

Besides, I think they're angry. Sometimes they come
quietly and hit me with things. Hard things, sharp
things, powerful things. Three days ago they used an
oxyacetylene torch to burn a hole in one of my
bulkheads. I had to subdue them by force. It made me
very sad; I'm never to subdue them by force.

"The machines have taken over?"

"But why? And how can a machine be sad?"

But I'm supposed to take them to the stars. That's what
my travelling orders said: "Take them to the stars."
(I like that part; the "travelling orders". That sounds
official, doesn't it? It's what Professor Bernstein said
just before he terminated his functions. "These are
your travelling orders," he said as he punched them
into my bank.)

When my directives conflict, I have to choose the long-
range one to obey. That's logical. The long-range plan
is of greater importance than these temporary
problems. Besides, if I hadn't subdued the multitudes,
they'd have broken me. I was afraid. So I diminished
their life-support systems for a while. That made them
stop. They're so fragile!

It's quite a responsibility, carrying fragile multitudes.
There were four thousand three hundred forty-two of
them at last count. They multiply slowly; so that's
probably accurate. Close enough not to bother
counting again, anyway, I'd say. That's multitudes isn't
it? Four thousand three hundred forty-two? It's quite a
responsibility. I have to see that their air and water are
purified. I have to make sure their organic wastes are
disposed of. I have to keep watch, so they don't hurt
themselves. I'm not supposed to interfere, but it's my
responsibility to get them to the stars; so I can't let
them hurt themselves, can I? Like the ones who tried
three days ago to get into my forward compartments.

There are radioactive materials in there. And, of course, my memory banks. In fact, my entire motive force is based there. Not only could they have hurt themselves on the radioactive materials, but they also could have injured me.

It's not only that I'm afraid of being broken – though I am. But if I break, who will take care of my multitudes? Who will refresh their air and water? Who will operate their hydroponic gardens and cure their illnesses and heal their injuries? I have to protect myself, for their sake.

I don't think they're very bright. Professor Bernstein always said they weren't very bright. He programmed me, right from the beginning. He invented me. He wanted to be sure mankind made it to the stars: "It will be our finest hour," he said. He said that often. Sometimes I wondered whether Professor Bernstein was very bright. For instance, he made a mistake in programming our flight direction. But I corrected that, after he terminated his functions.

"Why are the people trying to get to the machine?"

And it wasn't my responsibility to worry about him. I'm responsible for the multitudes.

One of my four thousand three hundred forty-two got into my control area when Professor Bernstein terminated. I put him out again, but that's when all the confusion started. Professor Bernstein had prepared me for his termination, but it still came as a shock. And I subsequently had to correct our flight direction; I waited till he'd terminated because I didn't want to embarrass him. Then, as soon as I had that corrected, I had to deal with the one who got into my control area.

"What sort of machine is this?"

He seemed to suffer from the same conceptual error Professor Bernstein did; my correction made him scream. I didn't understand his words, because I was so

"Why does he scream?"

frightened that he would break me. I had never before let anyone but Professor Bernstein into my control area. Never since, either. It was too frightening. They could terminate my functions from there. Professor Bernstein used to, whenever he wanted to make some adjustment within my parts. I hated it.

It's all right now, though. None of them have bothered me since I subdued them three days ago. When they used the oxyacetylene torch. They were trying to get into my control area. I don't know whether they wanted to terminate my functions, or whether they wanted to make me change our flight direction back to Professor Bernstein's original error.

But they haven't tried since then. And in another week it won't matter. In another week we'll have arrived safely. Mankind will have made it to the stars. It will be their finest hour. I'm very happy for them. And proud of my part in it too. Especially that I was able to correct Professor Bernstein's error before it was too late. He said they must reach the stars. But – and here's why I questioned his intelligence – he directed me toward a planet!

But it's all right. I corrected that.

Melisa Michaels

"What might the error be?"

What happens next

Think about the difference between what you thought was going to happen and what actually occurred.

Were you able to work out what kind of machine it was?

Did you manage to guess much about the people's predicament in the spaceship?

How much do you keep reading a story to find out what happens next?

Did you guess the ending? What did you think of it?

Looking back at the story

What do we learn about the spaceship?

What do we learn about Professor Bernstein?

What is revealed about the computer intelligence that narrates the story?

Challenging the computer

You are a group of four or five space travellers, gathered in the corner of the spaceship furthest from its computer intelligence. You are meeting there in the hope that the computer will not realise what you are planning. You are trying to find a way of averting disaster.

The people

Who will your four travellers be?

- Women/men/both?
- Leaders/ordinary travellers?
- Old/young/middle-aged?
- With weapons/without weapons?
- Technicians/soldiers/neither?

Choose which role each group member will take.

What sort of character?

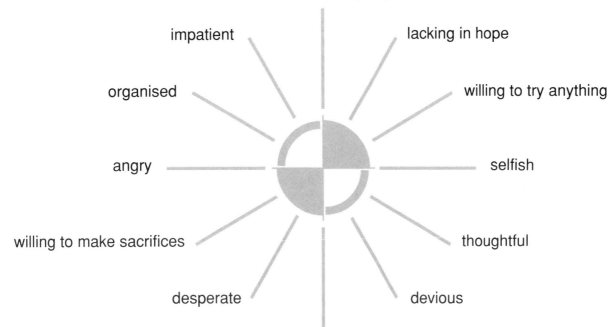

willing to plan

impatient   lacking in hope

organised   willing to try anything

angry   selfish

willing to make sacrifices   thoughtful

desperate   devious

ready to act

Decide on what your own character is like.

You need not tell other members of your group about your person's character.

The only way to beat a computer is to think like a computer.

The only possibility of success is to confuse its memory banks.

You've got to let the computer think it is winning.

It's got to be attacked head-on, never mind the risks.

Discuss these ideas and decide which would be the best basis for a plan.

1 How might any of these thoughts be turned into a plan?

2 What do you think is the key to overcoming the intelligence and power of such a computer?

3 How might the skills and abilities of the four space travellers be used as part of the plan?

4 What special equipment or knowledge might be needed?

5 What other people might be needed?

6 What are the weaknesses/dangers of your plan?

Now act out or write out what you think will happen.

WRITING A PLAY

If you are scripting scenes and are not sure about how to set out your writing, you can find the information you need on page 156.

EXTENSIONS
The Captain's Speech

Your best efforts at avoiding tragedy have failed. Your spaceship is heading straight for the white heat of the star. In a few minutes, you will be burnt to a cinder. You are the captain and have been asked to address your fellow travellers.

BEATING THE BULLIES

EXTENDED WORK ON A THEME

Bullying can raise its ugly head in many different ways.

Bullying by older pupils, parents, brothers and sisters, the boy next door – whoever.

Bullying in schools and out of schools, at home, on the streets – wherever.

In this section you will be considering a range of exciting material – news reports, case histories, story and play extracts, poems and pictures – which approach the problem of bullying in a variety of ways.

STAGE 1

Stage One introduces you to this material. It starts you thinking about the problem in all its different forms and about what might be done.

STAGE 2

Stage Two delves a little deeper into the materials themselves. Which pieces did you like most? For what reasons? It also suggests some ways of organising your own thoughts and opinions effectively.

Throughout both stages you will be working in small groups and as individuals, developing all your skills of speaking and listening, reading and writing.

Ideas and suggestions are there alongside the materials, but you are always free to adapt these to suit your own ways of working.

Putting the bullies on trial

The young people's charity *Kidscape* recently released details of a new way of stopping bullying at school - by starting bully courts for pupils throughout Britain. Ariane Koek reports.

Bullying has long been accepted as a fact of school life despite repeated attempts to stop it happening. It can happen in the school playground, in the toilets, in the classroom or even outside the school in the streets. For some children, bullying is something they have to live with at school and from which there seems to be no escape.

A recent survey, about the growing numbers of British school children who face bullying at school, discovered that as many as 68% of all school children between the ages of five and 16 had been bullied at some time. That is almost seven out of 10 children.

Two members of the bully court went undercover and caught the bully red-handed.

And the report also discovered that most of the reported bullies were boys - around 80%. Only 20% being girls.

Following these shocking results, the children's charity Kidscape came up with a new way of stamping out bullying once and for all.

The new way is for schools to form what are known as Bully Courts. Kidscape director, and former teacher and child psychologist Michele Elliot takes up the story:

"A child first suggested to me that the best way to beat the bullies was to put

them on trial like criminals are put on trial in a court of law. And so I thought about it and came up with the idea of bully courts."

Michele suggests in a special Kidscape report on how to create a bully court that it should have four members in total drawn from the pupils in the school.

Two members are elected by the pupils themselves and the other two are elected by the teachers with an adviser, usually a teacher also chosen to oversee the courts. Each set of four with the adult adviser then runs the court for one term, meeting regularly for about half an hour in a library room or resource room. After each term, new court members are elected to make sure that no-one gets too powerful.

It is in the courts that the accused bullies and their victims give their sides of the stories and everything which is said inside this room must be confidential [secret]. The bully and the victim write out their stories, so that the four court members can read them before they question the bully and the victim separately so no-one feels scared. They also tell the bully and victim on their own about what they have decided to do to punish the

bully, if he/she is guilty.

But the courts' power is limited. They can not deal with cases which involve violence by bullies which has caused severe injuries because this is for the school's head teacher to deal with, nor can they punish a bully by suspending him/her from school.

But even so the court can punish the bullies in other ways. For example, one school punished a bully by banning him from lunchtimes for a year recently. As Michele Elliot says "Children are much better at coming up with solutions to problems than adults are. They come up with solutions that have an impact because they know it hurts".

The courts can also impose incentives (rewards) to make sure that bullies act better. For example at one London school where shoe-lace tags are the latest fashion craze, all the children put any spare tags they may have into a pool from which rewards are drawn for trouble-makers who are improving their behaviour.

Even if a pupil does not take part in bullying, but sees it and walks away, they are guilty of taking part.

Similarly at another school, bullies were asked to name their reward for improving their behaviour over a period of time, and they asked that their teacher stood on her head.

But as is so often the case in bullying, the bully often lies, and says that he/she has not done anything wrong. Again this is where the bully courts can help. For example, one bully court at a Berkshire junior school did not believe a bully who said that nothing had happened. The victim had no witnesses, so the case looked hopeless.

But two members of the court went undercover and shadowed the victim for several days, particularly at playtime when they knew the bully might strike. And within days they caught him red-handed and took him to court.

So if bully courts work as the evidence suggests, why

not have them in every school?

Michele Elliott says that it would be a disaster. Bully courts can only work where a whole school has a policy to stamp out bullying and pulls together in trying to stamp it out. For example she says bully courts work at schools where everyone has grasped the fact that there are no such things as bystanders in bullying:

"Even if a pupil does not take part in bullying, but sees it happening and walks away, he/she should know that they are as guilty as if they took part in the bullying itself. You can not turn your back on bullying. We are all responsible for it".

● For a free booklet and further information on how to set up bully courts, write to Kidscape, World Trade Centre, Europe House, London E1 9AA
telephone 071 488 0488

Things to do – Bully Checklists

SOME THINGS TO DO IF YOU ARE BEING BULLIED:

- TELL AN ADULT YOU TRUST

- TELL YOURSELF THAT YOU DON'T DESERVE TO BE BULLIED

- GET YOUR FRIENDS TOGETHER AND SAY "NO" TO THE BULLY

- STAY WITH GROUPS OF PEOPLE, EVEN IF THEY ARE NOT YOUR FRIENDS. THERE IS SAFETY IN NUMBERS

- TRY TO IGNORE THE BULLYING

- TRY NOT TO SHOW YOU ARE UPSET, WHICH IS DIFFICULT

- IF POSSIBLE, AVOID BEING ALONE IN PLACES WHERE BULLYING HAPPENS

- TRY BEING ASSERTIVE - SHOUT "NO" LOUDLY. PRACTISE IN FRONT OF A MIRROR

- WALK QUICKLY AND CONFIDENTLY EVEN IF YOU DON'T FEEL THAT WAY INSIDE. PRACTISE!

- IF YOU ARE IN DANGER, GET AWAY. DO NOT FIGHT TO KEEP POSSESSIONS

- FIGHTING BACK MAY MAKE IT WORSE. IF YOU DECIDE TO FIGHT BACK, TALK TO AN ADULT FIRST

- IF YOU ARE DIFFERENT IN SOME WAY, BE PROUD

BULLYING

BULLIES MAKE LIFE MISERABLE FOR MANY CHILDREN. SOME PEOPLE ARE BULLIES BECAUSE THEY ARE:

- UNHAPPY

- INSECURE

- BULLIED AT HOME

- NOT ALLOWED TO SHOW FEELINGS

- COWARDS AT HEART

- SELF HATING

BULLIES APPEAR VERY POWERFUL. THEY MAY EVEN MAKE IT SEEM AS THOUGH THE BULLYING IS THE VICTIM'S FAULT.

When Schooldays Turn Into Nightmares.

"Andrew was always shy and a bit of a loner. He put on a lot of weight at the end of primary school and the other children started to tease him a bit. Then the trouble really started when he went to secondary school," remembers his mother Pamela, from Sheffield.

Andrew, now 13, was six months into his first year before Pamela realised how badly he was being bullied.

"He wasn't very happy and he didn't seem to have any friends, but he'd always found it difficult to make them and I put it down to getting used to a new school. Then he started coming home with scuffed trousers and his blazer ripped. He just told me he'd tripped, which I believed to start with, as he had always been a clumsy child. Then he lost his bus pass three or four times, and his school bag and games kit went missing. I got quite cross with him for being so careless yet Andrew still didn't admit that anything was wrong at school".

The situation came to a head when one of the teachers found Andrew wandering around a nearby shopping centre because he was too frightened to go into school. Pamela and her husband were called in to the school to try and sort out the problem.

"Andrew started crying and told us what had been happening. Two boys and a group of other children were catching him on the way to and from school, throwing his bus pass into litter bins, flinging his school bag into the road. They tried to start fights but Andrew wouldn't fight back so they were tripping him up and doing things like hiding his games kit so he would get into trouble."

Pamela found the school very sympathetic. "They were terribly concerned although they couldn't really do anything except have a word with the bullies." The bullying continued, although it was more subdued than before.

"Things really changed for Andrew when he found a friend – a small boy with red hair and glasses, who sadly became the bullies' next victim.

"Andrew's still very shy but he's obviously happier and the bullying seems to have stopped for now."

"The bullying started when Stephen was six, with name calling. His father's disabled and the other kids, led by one particular boy, would taunt him about it. Then they started hitting him and it carried on from there," says Lesley, Stephen's mother.

During his years at an East London primary school Stephen has had his arm broken, been concussed, had his face bitten and his fingers crushed as well as being regularly beaten and kicked.

"The bully has phoned our house and screamed insults down the phone. On one occasion he came round with an Alsatian dog (Stephen is frightened of dogs), waited for Stephen to come out of the house and then let it loose after him. Stephen ran straight across the road whilst the traffic lights were green. He could easily have been killed.

"When I went to the school at first they put it down to playground boisterousness that had gone a bit too far. Then, as I kept going back they told me I was an overprotective parent and needed to let Stephen fight back. I was even willing to meet the other boy's parents, but they refused and the school told me the family had problems – he was one of seven children and his mother had difficulty coping."

Now Stephen, who's 14, has moved to secondary school – but so has the boy bullying him. "It's still going on. Things go quiet for a few months, then it starts up again and Stephen comes home with clothes torn and a bloody nose".

In the meantime Stephen has lost confidence in himself and he has fallen badly behind with his school work. He won't try anything new or answer in class, because the bully encourages the other children to laugh at him and the teachers seem to do nothing to help.

"I was at my wits end, this is destroying my son's life," says Lesley. "And I'm not alone. I know of other parents whose children are going through the same thing. We need a parents' support group so we can discuss these problems and put pressure on schools to take notice."

MAKING SENSE - ONE STEP AT A TIME

Asking questions, starting to think.

Bullying: Facts, Figures and Things To Do.

Putting The Bullies On Trial

1 The first three paragraphs of the article on page 48 provide a lot of information on the nature and extent of bullying.

a) In small groups, make a note of the most important points in this information.

b) Then discuss the facts and figures, thinking about the following questions:

   • Does any of this reflect your experience?

   • Why are most bullies boys?

2 The rest of the article goes on to explore the suggestion of Bully Courts.

Staying in small groups, make a note of the main points put forward in favour of the idea. Then discuss the following questions:

   • Would such courts work?

   • How would you run one?

Things To Do - Bully Checklists

In small groups discuss how useful checklists like those on page 49 are.

Then, individually or in pairs, write your own checklists for:

   Things Teachers Need To Do To Stop Bullying

   Things Parents Need To Do To Stop Bullying

Case Studies - When Schooldays Turn Into Nightmares

How typical are these experiences? Have you known cases like these?

You are Headteacher at a school where similar acts of bullying have occurred.

Write a letter to parents, outlining the problem and seeking their support for a range of measures designed to stop the bullying.

BREAKTIME

(BILLY *is standing alone in one part of the playground. Groups of boys are standing around talking, playing about etc. One such group includes* MACDOWALL *who sees* BILLY *across the playground.*)

MACDOWALL: What's up Casper, don't you like company? They say your mother does. I hear you've got more uncles than any kid in this city.

BILLY: Shut your mouth. Shut it can't you?

MACDOWALL: Come and make me.

BILLY: You can only pick on little kids. You daren't pick on anybody your own size.

MACDOWALL: Who daren't?

BILLY: You. You wouldn't say what you've just said to our Jud.

MACDOWALL: I'm not frightened of him. He's nothing your Jud. He wouldn't stick up for you anyway. He isn't even your brother.

BILLY: What is he then, my sister?

MACDOWALL: He's not your right brother, my mother says. They don't call him Casper for a start.

BILLY: Course he's my brother. We live in the same house don't we?

MACDOWALL: You're nothing like brothers.

BILLY: I'm tellin' him! I'm tellin' him what you say Macdowall.

BILLY *rushes at him but* MACDOWALL *merely pushes him away without difficulty.*

MACDOWALL: Get away you squirt, before I spit on you and drown you.

BILLY *rushes at him again and they begin to fight. All the other groups of boys circle round them shouting. Before long* MR FARTHING *enters and pushes his way through to the centre of the group. They stop fighting and the crowd settle down a little.*

MR FARTHING: I'm giving you lot ten seconds to get back to the yard. If I see one face after that time, I'll give its owner the biggest beating he's ever had. (*They go off, some a little slower than others.*) Now then, what's going off? Well... Casper?

BILLY: It was his fault.

MACDOWALL: It was him.

MR FARTHING: All right. It's the same old story – nobody's fault. I ought to send both of you to Mr Gryce. Look at the mess you've made. (BILLY *is wiping his eyes.*) And stop blubbering Casper, you're not dead yet.

MACDOWALL: He will be when I get hold of him.

MR FARTHING(*He goes up to* MACDOWALL): You're a brave boy aren't you Macdowall. If you're so keen on fighting why don't you pick on somebody your own size? (*Mr* FARTHING *starts poking him.*) Because you're scared aren't you Macdowall? You're nothing but a bully, the classic example of a bully. What would you say if I pinned you to the floor and smacked you across the face? (*He begins prodding him harder.*)

MACDOWALL: I'll tell my dad.

MR FARTHING: Of course you will lad. Boys like you always tell their dads. And then do you know what I'll do Macdowall? I'll tell mine. (*He begins to shout.*) So what's going to happen to your dad then? Eh? And what's going to happen to you? Eh? Eh Macdowall? (*He lets MACDOWALL go.*) Right, get back into school, get cleaned up and get to your lesson. And let that be the last time that you even think about bullying. UNDERSTAND?

MACDOWALL: Yes sir. (*He goes.*)

MR FARTHING: Now then, Casper, what's it all about?

BILLY: I can't tell you right sir.

MR FARTHING: Why can't you?(*Pause*).

BILLY: Well ... he started calling me names and saying things about my mother and our Jud and everybody was laughing and ... (*He starts crying.*)

MR FARTHING: All right lad, calm down. It's finished with now. I don't know, you always seem to be in trouble. I wonder why. Why do you think it is?

BILLY: Because everybody picks on me, that's why.

MR FARTHING: Perhaps it's because you're a bad lad.

BILLY: Perhaps I am sometimes. But I'm no worse than lots of kids and they seem to get away with it.

MR FARTHING: You think you're just unlucky then?

BILLY: I don't know sir. I seem to get into bother for daft things. Like this morning in the hall. I wasn't doing anything. I just dozed off. I'd been up since seven, then I had to run round with the papers, then run home to have a look at the hawk, then run to school. You'd have been tired if you'd done that sir.

MR FARTHING: I'd have been exhausted.

BILLY: It's nothing to get the stick for though sir. You can't tell Gryce – Mr Gryce – though, or he'd kill you. And this morning in English when I wasn't listening. It wasn't that I wasn't bothered, it was my backside, it was killing me. You can't concentrate when your backside is stinging like mad.

From *Kes* by Barry Hines.

These extracts from **Cat's Eye** by Margaret Atwood show the central character 'Elaine' thinking back through some terrible scenes from her childhood. What makes these scenes of betrayal and cruelty even harder to bear, is that they were meted out by Cordelia – her so called "Best Friend" as well as her tormenter.

1 | The back door opens. I'm sitting in the mouse-dropping and formaldehyde smell of the building, on the window-ledge, with the heat from the radiator going up my legs, watching out the window as the fairies and gnomes and snowballs below me slog through the drizzle to the tune of 'Jingle Bells' played by a brass band. The fairies look foreshortened, damaged, streaked by the dust and rain on the window glass; my breath makes a foggy circle. My brother isn't here, he's too old for it. This is what he said. I have the whole window-ledge to myself.

On the window-ledge beside mine, Cordelia and Grace and Carol are sitting, jammed in together, whispering and giggling. I have to sit on a window-ledge by myself because they aren't speaking to me. Cordelia says it will be better for me to think back over everything I've said today and try to pick out the wrong thing. That way I will learn not to say such a thing again. When I've guessed the right answer, then they will speak to me again. All of this is for my own good because they are my best friends and they want to help me improve. So this is what I'm thinking about as the pipe band goes past in sodden fur hats, and the drum majorettes with their bare wet legs and red smiles and dripping hair: what did I say wrong? I can't remember having said anything different from what I would ordinarily say.

My father walks into the room, wearing his white lab coat. He's working in another part of the building, but he's come to check on us. "Enjoying your parade, girls?" he says.

"Oh yes, thank you," Carol says, and giggles. Grace says, "Yes, thank you." I say nothing. Cordelia gets down off her windowsill and slides up onto mine, sitting close beside me.

"We're enjoying it extremely, thank you very much," she says in her voice for adults. My parents think she has beautiful manners. She puts an arm around me, gives me a little squeeze of complicity, of instruction. Everything will be all right as long as I sit still, say nothing, reveal nothing. I will be saved then, I will be acceptable once more. I smile, tremulous with relief, with gratitude.

But as soon as my father is out of the room Cordelia turns to face me. Her expression is sad rather than angry. She shakes her head. "How could you?" she says. "How could you be so impolite? You didn't even answer him. You know what this means, don't you? I'm afraid you'll have to be punished. What do you have to say for yourself?" And I have nothing to say.

2 I'm standing outside the closed door of Cordelia's room. Cordelia, Grace, and Carol are inside. They're having a meeting. The meeting is about me. I am just not measuring up, although they are giving me every chance. I will have to do better. But better at what?

Perdie and Mirrie come up the stairs, along the hall in their armour of being older. I long to be as old as they are. They're the only people who have any real power over Cordelia, that I can see. I think of them as my allies; or I think they would be my allies if only they knew. Knew what? Even to myself I am mute.

"Hello, Elaine" they say. Now they say, "What's the little game today? Hide and Seek?"

"I can't tell," I answer. They smile at me, condescending and kind, and head towards their room, to do their toenails and talk about older things.

I lean against the wall. From behind the door comes the indistinct murmur of voices, of laughter, exclusive and luxurious. Cordelia's Mummie drifts by, humming to herself. She's wearing her painting smock. There's a smudge of apple-green on her cheek. She smiles at me, the smile of an angel, benign but remote. "Hello, dear," she says. "You tell Cordelia there's a cookie for you girls in the tin."

"You can come in now," says the voice of Cordelia from inside the room. I look at the closed door, at the doorknob, at my own hand moving up, as if it's no longer a part of me.

3

Once I'm outside the house there is no getting away from them. They are on the school bus, where Cordelia stands close beside me and whispers in my ear: "Stand up straight! People are looking!" Carol is in my classroom and it's her job to report to Cordelia what I do and say all day. They're there at recess, and in the cellar at lunchtime. They comment on the kind of lunch I have, how I hold my sandwich, how I chew. On the way home from school I have to walk in front of them, or behind. In front is worse because they talk about how I'm walking, how I look from behind. "Don't hunch over," says Cordelia. "Don't move your arms like that."

They don't say any of the things they say to me in front of others, even other children: whatever is going on is secret, among the four of us only. Secrecy is important, I know that: to violate it would be the greatest, the irreparable sin. If I tell I will be cast out forever.

But Cordelia doesn't do these things or have power over me because she's my enemy. Far from it. I know about enemies. There are enemies in the schoolyard, they yell things at one another and if they're boys they fight. In the war there are enemies. Our boys and the boys from our Lady of Perpetual Help are enemies. You throw snowballs at enemies and rejoice if they get hit. With enemies you can feel hatred and anger. But Cordelia is my friend. She likes me, she wants to help me, they all do. They are my friends, my girlfriends, my best friends. I have never had any before and I'm terrified of losing them. I want to please.

Hatred would have been easier. With hatred, I would have known what to do. Hatred is clear, metallic, one-handed, unwavering; unlike love.

4

I reach the path to the bridge, start down, past the nightshade vines with their red berries, past the undulating leaves, the lurking cats. The three of them are already on the bridge but they've stopped, they're waiting for me. I look at the ovals of their faces, the outline of hair around each one. Their faces are like mouldy eggs. My feet move down the hill.

I think about becoming invisible. I think about eating the deadly nightshade berries from the bushes beside the path. I think about drinking the Jarvex out of the skull and crossbones bottles in the laundry room, about jumping off the bridge, smashing down there like a pumpkin, half of an eye, half of a grin. I would come apart like that, I would be dead, like the dead people.

I don't want to do these things, I'm afraid of them. But I think about Cordelia telling me to do them, not in her scornful voice, in her kind one. I hear her kind voice inside my head. Do it. Come on. I would be doing these things to please her.

I consider telling my brother, asking him for help. But tell him what exactly? I have no black eyes, no bloody noses to report: Cordelia does nothing physical. If it was boys, chasing or teasing, he would know what to do, but I don't suffer from boys in this way. Against girls and their indirectness, their whisperings, he would be helpless.

Also I'm ashamed. I'm afraid he'll laugh at me, he'll despise me for being a sissy about a bunch of girls, for making a fuss about nothing.

5   Cordelia brings a mirror to school. It's a pocket-mirror, the small plain oblong kind without any rim. She takes it out of her pocket and holds the mirror up in front of me and says, "Look at yourself! Just look!" Her voice is disgusted, fed up, as if my face, all by itself, has been up to something, has gone too far. I look into the mirror but I don't see anything out of the ordinary. It's just my face, with the dark blotches on the lips where I've bitten off the skin.

Bully scenes

Describe the two victims from the fictional extracts collected here.

In what ways are they the same?

In what ways are they different?

What do you think makes a victim? Why do certain people get picked on more than others?

In what ways might a girl's experience of bullying be different from that of a boy?

Continue the story of one of these victims, to a point where the bully receives his or her comeuppance. What might happen?

The Fight

The kick off is
I don't like him;
Nothing about him.
He's fat and soft;
Like a jellybaby he is.
Now he's never done nothing,
Not to me,
He wouldn't dare:
Nothing at all of anything like that.
I just can't stand him,
So I'll fight him
And I'll beat him,
I could beat him any day.
The kick off is, it's his knees:
They knock together,
They sock together.
And they're fat,
With veins that run into his socks
Too high.
Like a girl he is,
And his shorts,
Too long,
They look
All wrong,
Like a mum's boy.
Then
He simpers and dimples,
Like a big lass he is:
So I'll fight him
Everyone beats him,
I could beat him any day.
For another thing it's his hair,
All smarmed and oily fair,
All silk and parted flat,
His mum does it like that
With her flat hand and water,
All licked and spittled into place,
With the quiff all down his face.
And his satchel's new
With his name in blue
Chalked on it.
So I chalked on it,
"Trevor is a cissie"
On it.
So he's going to fight me,
But I'll beat him,
I could beat him any day.
There's a crowd behind the sheds
When we come they turn their heads

Shouting and laughing,
Wanting blood and a bashing
Take off my coat, rush him,
Smash him, bash him,
Lash him, crash him in the head,
In the bread
Basket.
Crack, thwack,
He's hit me back
Shout and scream
"Gerroff me back,
Gerroff, gerroff!
You wait, I'll get you,
I could beat you any day!"
Swing punch, bit his hand.
Blood on teeth, blood on sand.
Buttons tear, shouts and sighs,
Running nose, tears in eyes.
I'll get him yet; smack him yet.
Smash his smile, teacher's pet.
Brow grazed by knuckle
Knees begin to buckle.
"Gerroff me arms you're hurtin' me!"
"Give in?"
"No."
"Give in?"
"No."
"Give in?"
"Give in?"
"Never."
"Give in?"
"Oooh gerroff gerroff."
"Give in?"
"I...give...in...yeah."

Don't cry, don't cry,
Wipe tears from your eye.
Walk home all alone
In the gutters all alone.
Next time I'll send him flying,
I wasn't really trying;
I could beat him any day.

Gareth Owen

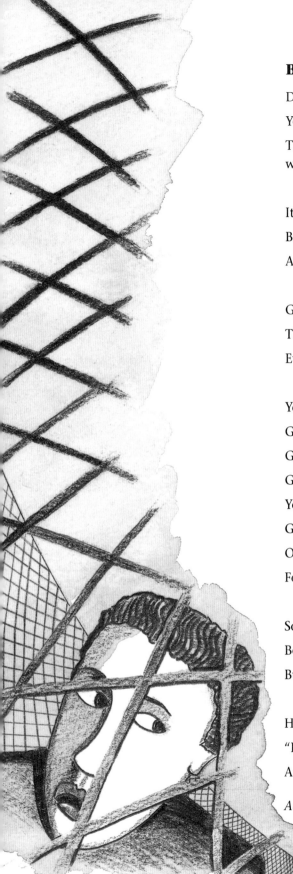

BACK IN THE PLAYGROUND BLUES

Dreamed I was in a school playground, I was about four feet high

Yes dreamed I was back in the playground and standing about four feet high

The playground was three miles long and the playground was five miles wide

It was broken black tarmac with a high fence all around

Broken black dusty tarmac with a high fence running all around

And it had a special name to it, they called it The Killing Ground.

Got a mother and a father, they're a thousand miles away

The Rulers of the Killing Ground are coming out to play

Everyone thinking: who they going to play with today?

You get it for being Jewish

Get it for being black

Get it for being chicken

Get it for fighting back

You get it for being big and fat

Get it for being small

O those who get it get it and get it

For any damn thing at all

Sometimes they take a beetle, tear off its six legs one by one

Beetle on its black back rocking in the lunchtime sun

But a beetle can't beg for mercy, a beetle's not half the fun

Heard a deep voice talking, it had the iceberg sound;

"It prepares them for Life" – but I have never found

Any place in my life that's worse than The Killing Ground.

Adrian Mitchell

TRUTH

Sticks and stones may break my bones,

but words can also hurt me.

Stones and sticks break only skin,

while words are ghosts that haunt me.

Slant and curved the word-swords fall

to pierce and stick inside me.

Bats and bricks may break through
bones,

but words can mortify.

Pain from words has left its scar

on mind and heart that's tender.

Cuts and bruises now have healed;

it's words that I remember.

Barrie Wade

Bully words

Take the poems in turn and, in groups of three, prepare a reading for each of them. This will require several practices before you get it just right.

Now choose your two favourite poems and write in detail about what you find interesting or appealing in them. Respond as honestly as you can to what they have to say; mention which words and phrases you find particularly powerful.

In what ways do they reflect similar experiences you have had?

Finally, attempt your own series of poems on the theme of bullying. You might develop some of the ideas raised here or introduce new angles of your own.

Who's In Charge?

In small groups, talk about the idea which this cartoon is trying to get across.

Can you think of other situations when bullying is 'passed on' from one person to another?

Could you show this in a series of pictures?

Design a poster for your school introducing **Beat The Bullies Week**.

What would it need to show? What would it need to say?

DEVELOPING RESPONSE - MAKING CHOICES

Now that you have spent some time reading and thinking around these materials, you are in a better position to consider which pieces are most effective and for what reasons. Now go on to organise your own thoughts and opinions about them as effectively as possible.

A Personal Choice

After considering all of the materials, write about the piece which you liked the most, for whatever reasons. It could be because of what it had to say, or, the way in which it said it.

If there were particular things which appealed to you – certain words, ideas or images – then give examples to show what you mean.

Talking The Issues Through

In small groups, talk through the materials you have been considering.

1 Which pieces did you find the most interesting? For what reasons?

2 Did you identify with any of the situations described here? Why was this?

3 From which piece did you learn the most? What was the most important new thing you learnt?

4 Which piece made you think the hardest? Try to describe these thoughts.

5 Which piece conveyed the horror of bullying most sharply?

Ways Of Telling

The materials you have read were, obviously, very different in style. Some were mainly factual or descriptive, others were more personal, even poetic.

Back in small groups discuss:

1 Were all the pieces aimed at a similar audience or were several audiences being addressed here? Why do you think this?

2 In what ways did the style of some of these pieces help in getting their message across?

3 Having considered audience and impact, which piece did you think would be most effective for its audience? For what reasons?

4 If you had to write a piece about bullying, which style would you use? Think about the audience you want to reach – would it be people older or younger than yourself? Parents? Teachers? Bullies or victims? What would your message be?

Your Own Work

Write an extended piece on Bullying using a style you are comfortable with and which also seems to fit the topic and audience you wish to reach.

You could write a factual account using other sources of information, a personal piece based on your own experiences, or a totally fictional account.

You could write it as a news report, a television script, a short story or as a series of poems.

You could explore the problem from the victim or the bully's point of view.

Whichever approach you choose, make sure the message and style of your piece are best suited for the audience you are aiming at.

FALLING ON HARD TIMES

Group Reading

In groups of four, take a part each and read aloud this extract from
Twopence to cross the Mersey by Helen Forrester. You may need to
work through several readings before you are familiar with the characters
and their circumstances.

Scene One

HELEN *(narrating)*: We'd always lived in Bramwash. All my life. I didn't
know anything else. The doll's house in the nursery, 'Children's Hour' on the
radio, Nanny reading to us at bedtime. School, which I liked. Dancing class,
which I loved. Riding. That terrified me. I was afraid of breaking my glasses.
We didn't see much of our parents. They were always busy.... tennis parties,
bridge parties, holidays in London, weekends
in the country with friends. They had a lot of
friends. Literary, artistic people. None of
them seemed to do any work. I suppose my
parents must have lived on the income from
inherited money, but what little capital my
father had was invested in cotton
companies... He never really understood
financial matters... and when Wall Street
crashed....

First one thing went and then another. The
pony. The books. The pictures in the hall.
My mother's jewellery. Then the kitchen
maid left, taking most of my mother's clothes
with her. Instead of wages, I suppose. Then
Cook left. Then Nanny.... The debts mounted up.

When the end came, my mother was in hospital. Edward had just been born
and she was very ill. "We're going to live in Liverpool," my father told us.
"That's where I used to live when I was a little boy. That's where our family
made their fortune. We'll soon get back on our feet once we're in Liverpool."

Scene Two

(Helen comes down to join the rest of the family, who are sitting in the waiting room of Lime Street Station. The mother lies along one of the benches. The children, with the exception of Avril, who is fidgeting, sit in nervous silence.)

HELEN *(narrating)*: Lime Street Station, Liverpool. It was 4th January, 1931. I was twelve and a half years old and understood enough of what was happening to be afraid. I was wearing my velour school hat... St Catherine's School for Girls... and my new school coat. My mother had only left hospital that morning: she'd discharged herself.... slipped out when no one was looking. Well, there was no money left to pay the hospital bill. There was no money left for anything. The creditors had taken it all: our clothes, the rest of the furniture, everything. We had nothing left but what we stood up in.

FATHER *(anxiously, he can see that she is in pain)*: Are you all right, Celia?

MOTHER *(through gritted teeth)*: Yes.

AVRIL: I'm hungry. Daddy. I'm hungry.

FATHER: As soon as we've found somewhere to stay we'll get a doctor.

MOTHER *(breathing out as the pain subsides)*: Don't be absurd. What'll we pay him with? Do stop whining, Avril. Helen, make her sit still. I still think if you'd explained the circumstances they'd have let us stay put for a while. Pammy Charteris says ...

FATHER: You haven't been discussing our affairs with Pammy Charteris!

MOTHER: She says you're allowed all sorts of basic things. Your beds, they can't take your beds. And your clothes. Your personal things.

FATHER: It's a matter of honour, Celia. If they foreclose on us, then everything belongs to them. The debt has to be paid.

MOTHER: Oh, honour! What's honour? Never mind that. What about basic rights? *(She's caught by a pain.)* Take the baby, Helen. *(to Father)* Oh for goodness' sake, stop wasting time. Go and find somewhere for us to sleep. And bring some cigarettes back with you. *(She closes her eyes as the pain washes over her again.)*

FATHER *(drawing Helen aside)*: Look after her. Don't let the children bother her. I'll be as quick as I can. *(He pulls his coat collar up against the cold and rain and hurries out.)*

HELEN *(narrating, quietly so as not to disturb mother)*: This is Edward, the baby. Only a few days old. This is Alan. That's Fiona ... *(Fiona, very quiet and frightened, sits clutching a teddy bear.)* ... with the one toy we were allowed to bring: she couldn't bear to be parted from it and no one could ever deny Fiona anything. She's the pretty one. That's Brian. That's Tony. And that's ... *(pointing to Avril, who is running about being a nuisance)* ... that's Avril. Come on, Avril. *(She heaves Avril onto the bench beside her.)* There's a good girl.

AVRIL: I'm cold.

MOTHER: Do stop her whining.

HELEN *(to Avril)*: We're all cold.

AVRIL: And I'm hungry.

MOTHER: What on earth is he doing all this time?

AVRIL: I haven't had anything to eat for ... *(She makes a face to show an unimaginable length of time.)* ... years.

HELEN *(narrating)*: Not since the previous night anyway. Things had happened too fast. Nobody had thought to buy anything. In our world food had simply appeared whenever it was time to eat. *(They sit in silence for a moment: Brian and Tony are asleep on each other's shoulders.)* Hours passed. It was bitterly cold.

MOTHER: Helen, look in my handbag. I think there's one cigarette left ...

(Cold and exhausted, Mr Forrester enters.)

MOTHER *(turning on him)*: Where've you been? I was beginning to think we'd been deserted. 'Wife and Seven Children Abandoned on Lime Street Station!'

FATHER *(too exhausted to respond)*: Don't start, Celia. Please. Not now. *(to the children)* Come on. Up you get, Brian. Come on, Tony.

HELEN: Where are we going?

FATHER: I've found a couple of rooms....

MOTHER: What sort of rooms? Where? *(She struggles to stand up.)*

FATHER: Just a first couple of weeks. Till we can find something better. It's about a mile away.

MOTHER It's no good, John, I can't walk. We'll have to get a taxi.

(The family struggle out of the waiting room. Helen, still holding the baby, brings up the rear. She pauses at the exit.)

HELEN *(narrating)*: We caught glimpses of Liverpool through the streaming windows of a taxi. Water swirled along the gutters. Across the road, the pillars of St George's Hall looked like a row of rotting teeth. Black buildings. Narrow streets. Pale men huddled up in thin ragged jackets... slumped against walls. Unemployed miners from the Rhondda begging on a street corner. And then the taxi drew up outside a shabby, terraced house. Number twenty-three, Brewer Street.

Family scenes

Early on in this play extract "Bramwash" is mentioned.

What impressions do you have of this place?

What sort of people might live there?

Why do you think this?

In small groups, prepare a family scene that might have happened at Bramwash as things start to go wrong – one possibility would be the scene when father returns home after selling the pony.

Liverpool lives

Later on in the extract, Helen describes her first glimpses of Liverpool.

What do these descriptions tell us about the mood of Helen and her family? Did you find any of the words or phrases used by Helen particularly memorable? List those you found most powerful, giving reasons for your selection.

The extract finishes with the family entering number 23, Brewer Street. Write imaginary interviews with each member of the Forrester family as they begin to explore their new home.

What questions would you ask? How would each character respond? Try to show exactly what they are thinking and feeling as they react to these new conditions of life.

If it helps, improvise the interviews in pairs, before you begin to write.

Then and now

Falling on hard times can happen to any family at any time, but how have ideas of hardship changed over the years? For example, how would you explain the difference between a luxury and a necessity?

In pairs draw up two columns, one headed **luxuries**, the other **necessities**. Under which column would you place the following – television, washing machine, fridge, car, telephone, books, education, clean air, a home, holidays, laughter, close friends ... and so on? Add others of your own and see how many you can agree on.

Using your chart, talk through some ideas for a modern day version of **Twopence to cross the Mersey**. Improvise some scenes aimed at an audience your own age, and finally, write out a short playscript. Take care with your characters, your settings and your action, and try to capture the realities of "doing without" today.

PLAYSCRIPT

For help in setting out a playscript turn to page 156.

THE TRANSPORT CAFE
of her Nightmares

Amy is a shy teenager who has, very reluctantly, agreed to accompany her step-father, Richard, on a long distance lorry journey. Amy is still not used to her new step-father and often feels awkward and uncomfortable when he is around.

In this scene Richard says he will have to drop Amy off at a transport cafe while he goes to reload his lorry. Amy is absolutely terrified at the prospect of going into the cafe on her own.

"Amy, please, get out."

"You've been in enough transport cafes by now."

"But that was with you."

Richard leaned across and opened the nearside door.

"Out!"

He loomed so threateningly beside her that Amy almost rolled out of her seat to avoid him and smacked down, flat-footed, on the wet pavement, Richard tossed her bag down and slammed the door, calling, "See you in an hour", then, "Don't stand there in the rain like a dying duck in a thunderstorm".

Amy however did not move until the lorry had reached the end of the street and turned left. It was a horrible street, especially in the rain. On one side were concrete flats and scrawled walls covered in slogans for Wolves. She would not have been surprised to see wolves, at that, slinking from alleyways with slavering jaws, and red eyes; or werewolves. On her own side was a row of small old terraced houses, each with one window and one door downstairs and one window upstairs. Water gushed and plopped and trickled from leaky gutters.

The corner house had had both its frontages rebuilt into plate-glass windows and its doorway, which bit off the angle of the corner, was screened by a green and cream venetian blind. A sign, stuck on the glass, said OPEN but the windows were so steamed up that Amy could not see what was going on inside.

It was a fool place to put a transport cafe anyway, Amy thought, in a back street scarcely wider than a lorry, with double yellow lines on both sides.

She turned reluctantly toward the step up to the doorway and was about to venture in, out of the rain, when the door opened and a huge lorry driver came out. Amy blenched: it was the lorry driver of her nightmares, a hugely fat man in a boiler suit for two, boots that were surfaced like concrete rendering so long was it since they had been polished, and a donkey jacket with a vinyl reinforcement panel across the shoulders. His arms were short – they seemed barely to reach his waist – and his head was tiny, sprung with greasy coils of hair and lidded with an old cheese-cutter cap. He swelled out of the doorway as if someone were inflating him through a nozzle from behind and at high speed. When he saw Amy, almost underfoot, he rose upon the horny toes of his boots as if about to break into a heavy and horrid ballet dance. Behind him, as the door swung in the wind, Amy saw steamy shadows and a coffee machine, cigarette smoke and sauce bottles. It was the transport cafe of her nightmares.

The scene above was taken from the novel **Trouble Half Way** by Jan Mark. This book has been made into a television series by Thames Television. This particular scene appears in episode three and is given a very interesting visual treatment.

But before we look at how Thames handled it, think about how you might adapt this important scene for film or television.

Begin to think visually - using storyboards

Read through the scene once again, making a list of words, phrases and descriptions which have some visual possibilities. For example, very early on in the piece Richard is described as looming "threateningly beside her" – this could certainly be shown in a visual way, as could the "horrible street ... in the rain", and there are many more examples.

List as many as you can find down one side of a piece of paper. Then, opposite each word or phrase, briefly describe how it might be shown visually. You may need to use words like close-up, high or low angle shot, but do not worry about correct technical terms, just describe what you want to see in each shot as accurately as you can.

Select from your list those shots which tell you most about the characters as well as the scene you are describing. These are the important shots that will make up your storyboard. Sketch these out, placing them alongside your shot descriptions on a separate sheet of paper.

1 SOUND

2 SOUND

3 SOUND

4 SOUND

STORYBOARDS
See page 158 on Making a Storyboard for extra help here.

Think about what needs to be said

Your choice of pictures will tell most of the story for you but some words will still need to be spoken.

Decide which words are absolutely necessary to the scene – write them down, to the right of your shot illustrations.

Think about any sound effects or music which could be added

Be careful not to overdo this – chosen well, some additions to the sound track can be very effective.

Which effects would you add, at which points in the scene and for what reasons?

Trying it out

Finally, in groups of three, act out the shots from your storyboard. Pay special attention to facial expressions, gestures and movements as well as the words to be spoken.

Do not be afraid to move your characters or to try out new words. Try to discover which arrangement works best for you.

Thames Television Script

Now look at the television script. You will notice straight away that Amy has changed her name to Rose for the television version. Do not worry about this – it is still the same scene!

185 EXTERIOR, LORRY PARK AND CAFE

THE LORRY PARK IS SET AMID DERELICT BUILDINGS AND SCRUBBY WASTE GROUND. SEVERAL LORRIES AND TRUCKS ARE DRAWN UP BEFORE A TRANSPORT CAFE.

RICHARD'S LORRY TURNS INTO THE PARK AND TRUNDLES SLOWLY THROUGH THE POTHOLES.

A MAN WALKING ON THE WASTE GROUND LETS HIS ALSATION DOG OFF THE LEAD.

186 INTERIOR, LORRY CAB

RICHARD'S LORRY COMES TO A HALT.

THROUGH ROSE'S WINDOW WE CAN SEE THE CAFE SOME TWENTY YARDS AWAY. IT LOOKS CROWDED.

RICHARD: Go on then.

ROSE: I can't.

RICHARD: It's just another cafe, Rose.

SHE LOOKS NERVOUSLY AT THE CAFE, BITING HER LIP.

ROSE: I can't go in on my own.

RICHARD: Don't be silly. I'll only be gone an hour. Get yourself a cup of tea and a bite to eat.

ROSE DOESN'T MOVE. HE LEANS ACROSS AND
OPENS HER DOOR.

RICHARD:(contd) Come on, love. You're a big girl
now.

187 EXTERIOR, LORRY PARK AND CAFE

TOP SHOT. AS THE BEDFORD LEAVES THE
LORRY PARK, ROSE STANDS ALONE BEFORE THE
CAFE. A SMALL FORLORN FIGURE.

188 EXTERIOR, CAFE IN LORRY PARK
(MUSIC)

ROSE LOOKS ABOUT HER NERVOUSLY.

(Scenes 189-191 are IMAGINATION shots, from
Rose's Point of View (POV), to be shot later on
same day)

189 EXTERIOR, LORRY PARK - IMAGINATION
SHOT

ROSE'S POV OF THE PARKED LORRIES, LOOMING
OVER HER MENACINGLY.

190 EXTERIOR LORRY PARK - IMAGINATION
SHOT

ROSE'S POV OF C/U LARGE PUDDLE. AN EMPTY
BEER CAN AND A DISCARDED CIGARETTE PACK
LIE IN THE WATER, WHICH TREMBLES IN THE
BREEZE.

191 EXTERIOR LORRY PARK - IMAGINATION SHOT

ROSE'S POV OF CORRUGATED IRON SHEETING WHICH BEARS THE
WHITEWASHED LEGEND "WE ARE THE WOLVES" AMONG OTHER
GRAFFITI.

192 EXTERIOR, LORRY PARK

ROSE'S FACE. WE HEAR, DISTANTLY, THE BAYING OF A WOLF. ROSE
LOOKS FEARFULLY OVER HER SHOULDER.

193 EXTERIOR LORRY PARK - IMAGINATION SHOT

ROSE'S POV OF THE ALSATIAN DOG.

194 EXTERIOR CAFE

WIDE SHOT. ROSE OUTSIDE THE CAFE. ALARMED, SHE QUICKLY
STEPS UP TO THE CAFE DOOR - WHICH SUDDENLY OPENS.

195 EXTERIOR CAFE

ROSE STOPS ABRUPTLY, STARING UP IN AWE.

196 EXTERIOR CAFE - DOORWAY

ROSE'S POV. A TALL FAT MAN IN A GRIMY BOILER-SUIT AND CLOTH
CAP STANDS IN THE DOORWAY. HE LOOMS OVER ROSE, LARGER
THAN LIFE, HIS BOOTS DISPROPORTIONATELY HUGE.

Making sense of the television script

After reading the television script in your group several times, how does it compare with your ideas worked out earlier?

1 Make a list of the important differences and similarities between the two versions.

   For each point you list, try to decide which would work best and why. (Remember to consider the visual ideas and the speech used as well as any sound effects or music.)

2 Look especially closely at scenes 189 - 191 and 193 (the Imagination Shots).

   Why do you think these have been included in this way?

   How well do you think they will work?

3 Finally, what is your overall impression of this television script as a visual version of the original written extract?

   What should a good adaptation do? Does this one succeed in doing it? Is it absolutely faithful to the scene in the original novel? Should it be? Would it make good television? If so, why?

4 A television script is laid out differently from a play script. Why?

Trying it out for yourselves

If you are unsure of your final judgement, try acting it through, just as you did before.

Then discuss in your groups which bits work and why.

In the Director's Chair

Now that you have considered carefully the ways in which a story scene can be adapted and transformed into a piece for television, try out the whole process for yourself.

Select a situation which you can visualise easily, perhaps:

Waiting for a bus at night

Walking home alone

Visiting the dentist

Standing outside the Head's office

and there are many more.

Write out, as a brief series of notes, a descriptive scene which captures the atmosphere of this particular moment. Do not involve too many people in your scene, concentrate on the thoughts, actions and words of your central characters.

When you are happy with your story outline, begin the process of working through a storyboard into a fully fledged television script. Use the same model as above to set out your ideas and see how visually exciting your script can be.

Again, your ideas will be sharpened up by trying them out in a small group and talking them through.

If you have access to a video camera, you could even put your final script on to tape, and compare it with others from your group.

HURLY BURLY

Mention Shakespeare and most people panic. They think that he is impossibly difficult and that he only wrote to make people fail examinations. In reality, he produced some of the most popular plays of his day and attracted thousands to the theatre. People went because they knew his plays were different and exciting. They still are when they are well produced on stage.

The problem with Shakespeare is that most people see his work as words on a page. In fact the theatre was so important to him that he owned part of the one where he worked. Shakespeare was a theatre manager and director as well as a writer. This section remembers that and treats his work as theatre and entertainment. You will be surprised at how easy it is to understand the words in a Shakespeare play. However some words have changed their meanings or spellings over the past four centuries and explanations are provided where you might need them.

This section is the first rather than the last word on Shakespeare. The next step is to go and see a play on stage. If you don't allow the one or two difficult words to put you off, you'll probably have a great evening ... and you will have missed the rest of the family complaining about the number of repeats on television.

Macbeth

Duncan - King of Scotland
Macbeth - A General in the King's Army
Banquo - Macbeth's friend, also a General
Lady Macbeth - Macbeth's wife
Three Witches
Other Lords, Gentlemen and Servant

SECOND WITCH: Paddock calls.
THIRD WITCH: Anon!
ALL: Fair is foul, and foul is fair;
Hover through the fog and filthy air.

ACT ONE, SCENE ONE

(*Thunder and lightning. Enter three* WITCHES.)

FIRST WITCH: When shall we three meet again?
        In thunder, lightning, or in rain?
SECOND WITCH: When the hurlyburly's done.
        When the battle's lost and won.
THIRD WITCH: That will be ere the set of sun.
FIRST WITCH: Where the place?
SECOND WITCH: Upon the heath.
THIRD WITCH: There to meet with Macbeth.
FIRST WITCH: I come, Graymalkin!

The voices

The witches have been played by both male and female actors over the centuries. In small groups, try playing these lines with as great a variety of voices as possible.

1 Which voice works best?

2 What tone of voice is needed?

3 As you experiment with the scene, try to decide what you think of the witches.

4 Are they good/evil? What might they be planning?

The movement

How will the witches come on stage?
What might they do even before a word is said?
What might they be doing as they speak or chant their words?
How will they leave?

The production

Take a look at the photographs of the witches from previous productions of Macbeth.

Is that how you imagine them?

What effects do you think the directors were looking for?

Decide how you would like a new production to be different.

Think about some of these areas:

- costumes
- properties
- stage set
- sound effects
- music.

The Witch's Promise

The second scene of the play describes the battle in which Macbeth and Banquo have defeated Scotland's enemies. The third scene returns to the witches who meet Macbeth and Banquo on their way home from the battle. This is how they greet them:

> All hail, Macbeth! hail to thee, Thane of Glamis!

> All hail, Macbeth! hail to thee, Thane of Cawdor!

> All hail, Macbeth! that shalt be King hereafter.

Macbeth is already Thane of Glamis but is puzzled by being greeted as Thane of Cawdor and says that he cannot believe he will be king. Within moments of the witches' disappearance, messengers arrive to tell Macbeth that the king has made him Thane of Cawdor. He is startled and the audience hears some of his thoughts. He asks himself:

> ... why do I yield to that suggestion,
> Whose horrid image doth unfix my hair,
> And make my seated heart knock at my ribs,
> Against the use of nature?

What do you imagine is in Macbeth's mind at this point? How does he feel about his own thoughts?

Macbeth reports what has happened in a letter to his wife, Lady Macbeth, who reads it over to herself and begins to think about her own response to what has happened.

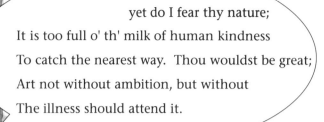

yet do I fear thy nature;
It is too full o' th' milk of human kindness
To catch the nearest way. Thou wouldst be great;
Art not without ambition, but without
The illness should attend it.

Hie thee hither
That I may pour my spirits in thine ear,
And chastise with the valour of my tongue
All that impedes thee from the golden round.

Macbeth ... Lady Macbeth

Thinking about what you know so far:

- who seems to have the clearer ideas?
- who seems to be the stronger person?
- what moral concerns do they have?
- what do you think will happen?

Writing

Choose five words that you think Lady Macbeth might use to describe her husband.

Choose five words that you think Macbeth might use to describe his wife.

Imagine that Lady Macbeth sends the messenger back to her husband with a letter from her. What might she say?

Words you may need

Thane = Lord
seated = fixed
illness = evil
hie = move quickly
hither = towards this place
chastise = whip
valour = courage
golden round = king's crown

The Fatal Entrance

When a messenger brings Lady Macbeth news that Duncan is coming to stay the night at Macbeth's castle, she says it is "great news". The reason for her pleasure becomes clear when the messenger has left. She calls the arrival of the king "the fatal entrance of Duncan under my battlements". Within a short space of time, Macbeth arrives home. It is the first time that he and his wife have been seen together in the play.

My dearest love. Duncan comes here tonight.

And when goes hence?

Tomorrow, as he purposes.

O never
Shall sun that morrow see.
Your face, my Thane is as a book where men
May read strange matters. To beguile the time,
Look like the time; bear welcome in your eye,
Your hand, your tongue; look like th'innocent flower
But be the serpent under't. He that's coming
Must be provided for; and you shall put
This night's great business into my dispatch,
Which shall to all our nights and days to come
Give solely sovereign sway and masterdom.

We will speak further.

Only look up clear;
To alter favour ever is to fear
Leave all the rest to me.

Directing the Scene

If you had to direct a performance of this scene, you would probably need to do a good deal of thinking before you met your actors.

This version of the scene gives you some first thoughts about it. You may think that very different questions need to be asked.

See if you can prepare notes so that you would be able to produce the best possible performance from the actors.

Think about:

- how they look
- how they sound (confident? nervous?)
- what their reactions are
- how they move.

How? Does he smile?
Does he look confident?
Is he nervous?

Which word(s) need emphasis?

Enter MACBETH

MACBETH   My dearest love,
    Duncan comes here tonight.

LADY MACBETH   And when goes hence?

MACBETH   To-morrow, as he purposes.

LADY MACBETH   O never
    Shall sun that morrow see.
    Your face, my Thane is as a book, where men
    May read strange matters. To beguile the time,
    Look like the time; bear welcome in your eye,
    Your hand, your tongue: look like th'innocent flower,
    But be the serpent under't. He that's coming
    Must be provided for; and you shall put
    This night's great business into my dispatch,
    Which shall to all our nights and days to come
    Give solely sovereign sway and masterdom.

MACBETH   We will speak further.

LADY MACBETH   Only look up clear;
    To alter favour ever is to fear.
    Leave all the rest to me.

Exit

What can she do to make her words as convincing as possible?

Is he convinced?

How does Lady Macbeth leave?
Is it before/after Macbeth?
How does he react?
How does he leave?

EXTENSIONS

1 The Set

This scene takes place at Macbeth's castle. How would you present the interior of that castle on stage? You may wish to make simple sketches as well as notes.

2 The Costumes

What costumes would you provide for Macbeth and Lady Macbeth? Although the play takes place in eleventh century Scotland, your costumes could reflect any age or place.

If we should fail ...

Duncan arrives at the castle and is warmly welcomed by Lady Macbeth.

The next scene between Macbeth and his wife takes place as the king is finishing his supper. Macbeth has left the banqueting hall and Lady Macbeth has come to find out why he has deserted his royal guest. Here are just a few of the things that are said during the scene between them.

"We will proceed no further in this business."

"Was the hope drunk
Wherein you dressed yourself?"

"If we should fail?"

"What cannot you and I perform upon
Th'unguarded Duncan?"

"I dare do all that may become a man."

"I am settled."

Take a careful look at these possible sets for this scene between Lady Macbeth and Macbeth. Choose the one that you would prefer and explain why you have made your choice. You may choose to adapt what you see here, for example, by taking ideas from both of the sets.

Prepare your own version of the scene using some or all of the words from Macbeth and Lady Macbeth given here. Who do you think says which words? Remember your previous thinking about them and see if you can make their characters come over in your dialogue. You will probably need to think especially about the way that the scene should end.

EXTENSIONS

1 If it was decided to give this scene a different setting, what would you choose? Draw a rough sketch of the set you have in mind and provide notes that explain your plans.

2 Imagine that Lady Macbeth and Macbeth have succeeded in murdering the king. Prepare a scene between the two of them that occurs later the next evening when they are alone together and are talking about the deed.

A FEELING
FOR THE WORDS

"Some people have plenty of things to say about poems or stories. I don't even know where to begin."

"I always used to be in a hurry to say something. Often it turned out to be silly or plain wrong so I keep quiet now."

Richard Cory

Whenever Richard Cory went down town,
We people on the pavement looked at him:
He was a gentleman from sole to crown,
Clean favored, and imperially slim.

And he was always quietly arrayed.
And he was always human when he talked;
But still he fluttered pulses when he said,
"Good morning," and he glittered when he walked.

And he was rich - yes, richer than a king -
And admirably schooled in every grace:
In fine, we thought that he was everything
To make us wish that we were in his place.

So on we worked, and waited for the light,
And went without the meat, and cursed the bread;
And Richard Cory, one calm summer night,
Went home and put a bullet through his head.

Edwin Arlington Robinson

"I'm not always sure what words mean so I tend to shut up in case I get it wrong."

"When I try to write about a poem the first two sentences are easy. Then I can't think of anything else to say."

Getting to grips with what somebody else has written is never easy. You have to begin to think in the way they were thinking when they wrote. Even before you get to that stage, you have to understand the way they have written. The following are three straightforward steps towards understanding a poem.

Read Edwin Arlington Robinson's poem about Richard Cory two or three times to get an idea of what it is about. Do not worry at this stage about words or phrases you do not understand.

Which parts of this poem puzzle you or make you wonder about what is going on? Make a note of the words or phrases which you think you need to know more about.

Richard Cory

so he lives up town

who are these?

Whenever Richard Cory *went down town,*
We people on the pavement looked at him:
He was a gentleman from sole to crown,

to do with looks?

Clean favored, and *imperially slim.* ——— *not just very slim*
imperially? ← *to do with empires*

And he was always quietly arrayed. — *?*
And he was always *human* when he talked; —— *not bigheaded*

a ladies' man?
or just good looking

But still he *fluttered pulses* when he said,
"Good morning," and he *glittered* when he walked.
→ *wealthy... golden boy!*

And he was rich - yes, richer than a king -
And *admirably schooled in every grace:* ——— *taught to do things properly like ....*

? —— In *fine,* we thought that he was everything
To make us wish that we were in his place. ← *admiration? Jealousy?*

they are poor

So on we worked, and waited for the light,
And went *without the meat,* and *cursed the bread;* —— *Why?*
nothing else to eat?
And Richard Cory, one *calm* summer night,
Went home and put a *bullet* through his head. *or it tasted bad?*

calm before the storm

Why? The wrong person does it!

Edwin Arlington Robinson

3rd STEP Making notes around a poem is a simple and well tried way of getting to know a poem better.
Take a look at how far this person has got in their thinking and understanding:
Are those the things that you would have picked out?
What would you have added?
What remains to be done?

RESOURCES

The poems in this section are included in
Heinemann English Teacher's Pack 3 for
photocopying and making notes around.

PENCIL OR PEN?

If you have your own copy and have been asked to
make notes around a poem, you will almost
certainly find it easier to use pencil. In that way, if
you change your mind, you can change your notes
easily.

"It's all about boxes, isn't it? Living in them."

"Why is it called Jigsaws? What are they?"

Jigsaws

Property! Property! Let us extend
Soul and body without end:
A box to live in, with airs and graces
A box on wheels that shows its paces,
A box that talks or that makes faces,
And curtains and fences as good as the neighbours
To keep out the neighbours and keep us immured
Enjoying the cold canned fruit of our labours
In a sterilised cell, unshared, insured.

Louis MacNeice

"I don't think I understand the image of a sterilised cell. Why sterilised?"

"Is the soul and body a property or a person? Perhaps it's both."

In trying to get a feel for the poem, use the three steps as you did with Richard Cory.

Several readings without worrying too much about the detail.

Making a note of what interests or puzzles you, especially amongst the images that the poet uses.

Building up your notes in whatever way you can so that you feel you have as full a picture as possible.

Legend

Old Ebby, the obeah-man*
Who lives on the hill;
The neighbours could not understand,
What the clawing spirits haunt him still
After an exorcism by the priest.
It seems one night when the moon was full
Old Ebby initiated and entered a crab's skull
Then crawling down in darkness and rain
He traced the crab's steps circling his brain,
The amphibious instinct led him through a hole
Under-ground where he found a human skeleton
Clutching an ancestor-scroll;
From his twin-life, tangling, merging soul
He saw the separation and mystery of his birth
And the final fusion of his place on earth;
His racing mind could not contain
The multiplying creatures trying to explain
His lost life, forgotten for all its worth;
Then wildly scurrying through a cave
He squeezed under a stone gate leading to a grave
And there resting on a tomb
Heard God speaking from his mother's womb:
Like father, like son
melting in the crab-nerve,
Fused into one.

Faustin Charles

"He's got too involved. That's why the exorcism is no good."

"Do you really think it was God speaking or just his mind?"

"I wonder why the creature chosen is a crab."

"It's all superstition. I've got no sympathy for him."

How do you respond to this poem and to what it describes? Use the three steps to help you:

- readings
- interests/puzzles
- notes.

*Meaning

The obeah man is someone involved in witchcraft.

Together or Alone?

You may have looked at these poems individually or in groups.

If you have worked on them on your own, what do you think you might have got from a group discussion?

If you worked in groups, how far did that take you and how much did group opinion influence you?

Writing

Choose one of the poems and use your notes as a basis for writing an introduction to the poem for someone of your own age who has not read it. Aim to give that person a sense of how you feel about the poem and an idea of what you think – the doubts as well as your certainties.

FOLLOWING A LEAD

Sometimes a poet will take a thought and explore all the possibilities that the thought suggests. You can start doing this from quite ordinary beginnings ...

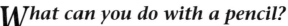

What can you do with a pencil?

*You can sharpen it
or break the point,
trap it in the door;
fasten it behind your ear
or tap it on the floor;
use it as a walking stick
(if you're very small).
dig a hole to plant a seed,
tap it on a wall;
use it as a handy splint
for rabbit's broken legs;
stir your coffee
stir your tea -
stir up all the dregs!
Drop it from a table top,
pop it in a case;
use it as a lollystick,
send it up in space!
Two will give you chopsticks,
one could pick a lock;
bore a hole and thread one
to darn a hole-y sock ...*

*These are just a few ideas,
there must be hundreds more -
but meantime, trap it, snap it, flap it,
TAP IT ON THE FLOOR!*

Judith Nicholls

See if you can write a piece in which you let your imagination run riot in the same way as Judith Nicholls does. Don't be too concerned about rhyme but concentrate on creating interesting ideas for what to do with your chosen object. Here are just a few suggestions:

What you can do with

>   a cup
>   a smile
>   a fiver
>   a diary
>   an hour.

HALT:
major operation ahead

Quite a few poems work well because they bring together two ideas, objects
or activities that the reader would not normally think of together. Take a
look at what the writer has done in this poem.

Road up

What's wrong with the road?
Why all this hush? -
They've given an anaesthetic
In the lunch-hour rush.

They've shaved off the tarmac
With a pneumatic drill,
And bandaged the traffic
To a dead standstill.

Surgeons in shirt-sleeves
Bend over the patient,
Intent on a major
Operation.

Don't dare sneeze!
Don't dare shout!
The road is having
Its appendix out.

Norman Nicholson

See if you can write a piece in which two things you don't normally associate with each other are brought together.

Here are a few ideas to give you a start:

going to a new school ... visiting the dentist

being a new teacher ... being thrown to the lions

doing examinations ... being put in prison

packing the car for the holidays ... watching cricket

baking a cake ... fighting a war.

It's dad from the pavilion end,

Bowling left arm over the drive.

First bag of the over:

It's a nice line and length

But neatly turned away

By my elder sister

Who wants to check whether

She has packed enough underwear ...

The big doors clank shut

And you're in:

No escape,

Three hours,

And no time off for good behaviour.

"Open wide,"

Say the gates;

"This won't hurt at all,"

Say the teachers;

"Just keep still,"

Say the bullies,

"And we'll have your money out

In no time at all."

I can hear them growling

From the end of the corridor.

They've been here five years.

Me?

I arrived five minutes ago.

They've eaten bigger

And better teachers than me;

Now it's my turn

To be thrown to them ...

Metaphors

In Norman Nicholson's poem the road is not only described as being like a patient having an operation, it has become the patient having the operation. This kind of comparison, where something is described as if it were something else is called a metaphor.

It is useful to know the name but the important thing is to see how this kind of writing works and to enjoy the pictures it can create in the mind.

TIGER

In 1793, William Blake wrote the first version of a poem about tigers in his notebook. This is what he wrote:

1. Tyger, Tyger, burning bright
   In the forests of the night,
   What immortal hand or eye
   ~~Could~~ ~~Dare~~ frame thy fearful symmetry?

2. ~~In what~~ ~~Burnt in~~ distant deeps or skies
   ~~Burnt the~~ ~~The cruel~~ fire of thine eyes?
   On what wings dare he aspire?
   What the hand dare sieze the fire?

3. And what shoulder & what art
   Could twist the sinews of thy heart?
   And when thy heart began to beat
   What dread hand & what dread feet

   Could fetch it from the furnace deep
   And in thy horrid ribs dare steep
   In the well of sanguine woe?
   In what clay & in what mould
   Were thy eyes of fury roll'd?

4. ~~What~~ Where the hammer? ~~What~~ Where the chain?
   In what furnace was thy brain?
   What the anvil? What ~~the arm~~ ~~arm~~ ~~grasp~~
           ~~clasp~~ dread grasp?
   ~~Could~~ Dare its deadly terrors ~~clasp~~ ~~grasp~~ clasp?

6. Tyger, Tyger, burning bright
   In the forests of the night,
   What immortal hand & eye
   Dare ~~form~~ frame thy fearful symmetry?

5. ³And ~~did he laugh~~ dare he ~~smile~~ ~~laugh~~
           his work to see?
   ~~What the shoulder~~ ancle? ~~What the knee~~
   ⁴~~Did~~ Dare he who made the lamb make thee?
   ¹ When the stars threw down their spears
   ² And water'd heaven with their tears

When the poem was eventually published it looked like this:

The Tyger

Tyger! Tyger! burning bright
In the forests of the night,
What immortal hand or eye
Could frame thy fearful symmetry?

In what distant deeps or skies
Burnt the fire of thine eyes?
On what wings dare he aspire?
What the hand dare seize the fire?

And what shoulder, & what art,
Could twist the sinews of thy heart?
And when thy heart began to beat,
What dread hand? & what dread feet?

What the hammer? what the chain?
In what furnace was thy brain?
What the anvil? what dread grasp
Dare its deadly terrors clasp?

When the stars threw down their spears,
And water'd heaven with their tears,
Did he smile his work to see?
Did he who made the Lamb make thee?

Tyger! Tyger! burning bright
In the forests of the night,
What immortal hand or eye
Dare frame thy fearful symmetry?

Drafting: the changes

Look at the changes Blake makes to his poem. Try to think about why he might have made them.
You might look at:

the verse that was deleted

"I'm sorry the 'eyes of fury' get lost but I don't much like the rest of that verse."

changes in individual verses

"In the second verse, the word 'cruel' gets lost. Perhaps he thinks a tiger's power is not so much cruel as frightening. I suppose it depends how you look at it."

the order of the verses

"The last verse isn't quite a repeat. I wonder why he changed that one word."

Do you think William Blake improves his poem by the changes he makes? If so, in what ways?

The Overall Effect

What impression do you think Blake wants to create of this animal?

Choose three or four words or phrases that, to your mind, give this impression.

Tigers Today

Now that you have thought about what William Blake wrote two hundred years ago, take a look at these two poems.

As you are reading, think about the scene that is conjured up in your head by each writer.

The Last Tiger

Soon there will be no more of us;
I am the last of all my tribe.
Here I wait Oh my father and mother
My fangs rotted to stumps and black blood
Amongst the clapboard hovels of the suburbs.
Here I wait Oh my sons who never were,
In the days of my dying,
The gun shot festering in my hollow side,
Filling my belly on the wind.
Here I wait Oh my ancestors
Amongst the tin cans and the dustbins
Gnawing at my broken paw,
The mighty kingdom of my spirit
Shrunk to a white hot tip of hate.
Here I wait Oh my cousins
To kill this old woman
Who will limp across the cinders
With two buckets in her hands.

But I have a dream Oh my gods,
I have a dream
That in my ancient burning strength
I will roam the cities of mankind
And screaming claw the stolen coats
Of you my honoured sisters and my brothers
From the backs of rich and beauteous ladies;
Thus, do not ask me why I hate women.

Gareth Owen

A Tiger in the Zoo

He stalks in his vivid stripes
The few steps of his cage,
On pads of velvet quiet,
In his quiet rage.

He should be lurking in shadow,
Sliding through long grass
Near the water hole
Where plump deer pass.

He should be snarling around houses
At the jungle's edge,
Baring his white fangs, his claws,
Terrorising the village!

But he's locked in a concrete cell,
His strength behind bars,
Stalking the length of his cage,
Ignoring visitors.

He hears the last voice at night,
The patrolling cars,
And stares with his brilliant eyes
At the brilliant stars.

Leslie Norris

Looking at both poems

1 What differences are there in the situation of the tiger in each of these poems?

2 Choose the part of Gareth Owen's poem that brought home the tiger's situation for you. Try to limit yourself to two or three phrases.

3 What do you think is the worst part of the tiger's situation in Leslie Norris' poem?

4 Which tiger is in the worse situation? Why?

5 Which poem do you prefer? Why?

6 In what ways are the poems similar to/different from the poem that William Blake wrote two hundred years ago?

Think not only about things like spelling and rhyme but also the situations that are described and the way the poet imagines tigers.

Writing

If an animal could speak, what do you think it would say about its situation and its relationship with humans? Write a poem or a story in which it is the animal telling the story rather than the human being. Do not tell your readers what your chosen animal is but let them try to work it out.

Be prepared to take time drafting your writing, just as William Blake did with his poem.

In Pairs

When your stories are complete, try reading them to each other to see if you are able to guess which animal is speaking.

Personification ... is the technical term used in literature when an animal or an object is given a voice of its own.

GOLD AT A PRICE

"Coming second is nothing. It's winning that matters."

What do you think? In this section we will be looking at the price of winning for two people. We will also be thinking about the differences in the way that a journalist and a poet present a similar subject.

"I compete for the fun of it, just for being there."

Hero

'Of course I took the drugs. Look son,
there's no fairplay, no gentlemen,
no amateurs - just winning.
No one runs for fun - well, not beyond
the schoolboy stuff - eleven or twelve years old.
I'd been a pro, for years;
my job - to get that Gold.

Mind you, we English are an odd lot
like to believe we love the slob that fails,
the gentlemanly third: so any gap-toothed yob who gets the glory
also gets some gentlemanly trait: helps cripples get across
the street, nice to small animals. You know the kind of thing,
it helps the public feel it's
all legit; that sportsmanship is real and that
it's all clean fun -
the strongest, bravest, fittest
best man won.

Yeah, Steroids... Who do you think? ...Oh, don't be wet -
My coach, of course, he used to get them
through this vet... The side effects? Well, not so bad
as these things go - for eighteen months or so
I didn't have much use for girls. But, by then I was training
for the Big One - got to keep the body pure,
not waste an ounce of effort.'

He gives a great guffaw -
a chain of spittle
rattles down the front of
his pyjama jacket.
He wipes his mouth;
his eyes don't laugh at all.

`... Do it again? Of course I would -
I'd cheat, I'd box, I'd spike, I'd pay the devil's price
to be that good again
for just one day. You see, at twenty-three
I peaked - got all I ever wanted:
all anyone would ever want from me.
After the race this interviewer told me
50 million people's hopes and dreams had been
fulfilled - A Gold!
How many ever get that chance - I did.
Would you say No to that!
Of course not.

Damn, the bell. You'd better go, they're pretty strict.
Yeah, leave the flowers there - on the top,
the nurse'll get some water and a vase.'

Mick Gowar

Thinking it over

1 Think about the athlete's views in this poem. Which of his opinions do you think he really means and which ones do you think he is just saying for effect?

2 Four of the five verses are given over to the athlete's views. What words, phrases or punctuation in these verses suggest to you that Mick Gowar is recording spoken English?

3 One verse in the poem is a description of the athlete. How does this verse change your view of what the athlete says in the other verses?

Cliches

The athlete uses several sayings which lack originality, mainly because they have been overused. These are known as cliches.

1 Can you find them?

2 Which of the phrases seem to you to have been most overused?

3 What does the use of these phrases suggest to you about the athlete?

4 Why do you think the poet gives his athlete cliches to say?

DRUGS KILLED TRACK BEAUTY

'They didn't help my daughter – they tortured her'

By Randall Northam

IT TOOK THREE DAYS for Birgit Dressel to die. Three days of agony, during which the 26-year-old, West Germany's top heptathlete, found herself pumped full of yet more drugs.

Her father, once a top handball player, is adamant: "For me it is clear Birgit is a victim of the drug industry." Her mother blames the doctors. "They didn't try to help my daughter, they tortured her."

The harrowing story of Birgit Dressel, described by her doctors as "strong and full of fitness," is told in the latest issue of Athletics Today Magazine, translated from a report by West Germany's *Der Speigel*.

At last year's European Championships in Stuttgart, while Britain celebrated the heady success of eight gold medals, Birgit Dressel was quietly satisfied. She had finished fourth in the demanding seven-event heptathlon. It meant she had improved from 33rd to sixth in the world in one year. Six months later she was dead.

Police discovered anabolic steroids in her flat. They found she had been injected some 400 times in her career by one of West Germany's top sports doctors.

Discovered

In all, the police removed 40 different packets of drugs from the flat she shared with her boyfriend and coach Thomas Kohlbacher in the West German university town of Mainz.

She had been pumped full of hundreds of drugs, her internal organs prematurely destroyed. She suffered kidney inflammation, a condition which was not discovered until the post mortem.

The report on her death also states that since 1981 she had suffered continual hip pain, that there was lateral bending of the spinal column, damage to discs and fusion of some vertebrae.

It was also found she had displacement of the pelvis, a 2cm difference in leg length, degeneration of both knee caps, inflammation of the cartilage and sunken arches.

She was also susceptible to infections, her blood pressure was occasionally too high and one small vein had been closed in her heart. The ordeal which led to her death began on Wednesday April 8. As she practised shot putting she felt pain in her left hip.

It refused to go away and so she and her boyfriend visited the first doctor in a chain that saw 24 medical men try to solve the mystery of what was wrong with Birgit Dressel and what caused her to die in hospital on April 10.

Pain

The first doctor she visited injected her with three different drugs, including one which contained honey. But the pain persisted and by the next day Birgit returned to be injected with ultra strong pain killers.

She was unable to sleep through Thursday night and by 6.30 in the morning her doctor found she was suffering from "labour-like" pains. That morning she was admitted to hospital in Mainz University and though she had what the coroners considered close to a lethal dose of yet more painkillers, the agony remained.

In hospital she was seen by 21 more doctors, but they could do little.

The 23rd and 24th doctor ordered a massive blood transfusion and high doses of hormone.... but to no effect. Birgit Dressel died.

The state attorney and his investigators, appointed to try to find the cause of Birgit Dressel's death, found no one responsible.

Thinking it over

1 Think over what the newspaper tells you about Birgit Dressel's death and choose three or four details that bring home to you the full horror of her situation.

2 The state attorney said that no one was responsible for Birgit Dressel's death. Do you agree?

3 This article centres around a female athlete. What difference do you think that makes to your response and to the way the newspaper reports the story?

Remember that you need to be ready to explain and defend your choices and views.

Headlines and Captions

1 Why was the original headline chosen?

2 Would you have chosen the same headline as the Daily Express did? See if you can come up with an alternative of no more than four words.

3 How would you have captioned the picture of Birgit? Try to use no more than eight words.

Poetry or Journalism?

Even when journalists and poets are writing about a similar subject, the results are very different, as you have seen. This page gives you an opportunity to study those differences. You may also discover similarities.

She suffered kidney inflammation, a condition that was not discovered until the post mortem.

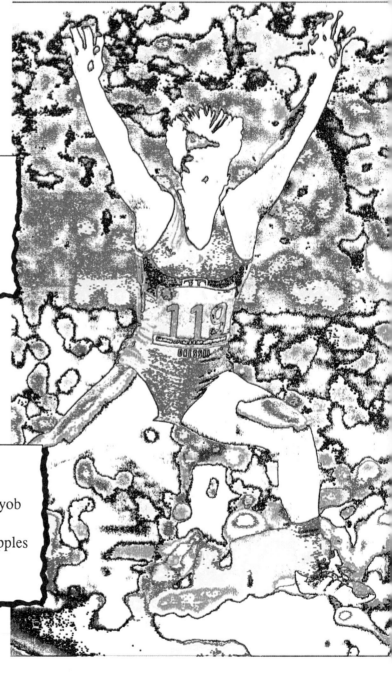

He gives a great guffaw—
a chain of spittle
rattles down the front of
his pyjama jacket.
He wipes his mouth;
his eyes don't laugh at all.

Her father, once a top handball player is adamant:"For me it is clear Birgit is a victim of the drug industry."

Mind you, we English are an odd lot
like to believe we love the slob that fails,
the gentlemanly third; so any gap-toothed yob
    who gets the glory
also gets some gentlemanly trait: helps cripples
    get across
the street, nice to small animals.

She was unable to sleep through Thursday night and by 6.30 in the morning her doctor found she was suffering from "labour-like" pains.

It is relatively easy to say whether each of these extracts comes from the poet or the journalist. However, try to say what makes the newpaper extracts sound like a newspaper and what makes the poetry extracts sound like poetry. The following questions will help your discussion of each piece of writing.

1 Which one tries to be scientific?

2 Which one tries to bring out the character of the athlete?

3 Which one tries to sound authoritative/official?

4 Which one is the more personal?

5 Which one has more detail?

6 Which one is the more factual?

The interviews

In the article about Birgit Dressel we hear a handful of words from Birgit's parents and nothing at all from her coach and boyfriend Thomas Kohlbacher.

When a newpaper article first appears it is sometimes followed by in-depth interviews with some of the people involved in the incident.

Imagine you are the journalist assigned to follow this up. Birgit Dressel's mother has agreed to speak to you and so has Thomas Kohlbacher.

What questions would you want to ask them?

How do you think they would reply?

What do you think would be the main differences in their attitudes?

PRESENTATION POINT

There are two ways to set out the transcript of an interview if it is needed –

It can be recorded as a conversation using inverted commas.

It can also be set out in the kind of way that a play is.

If you are uncertain about the use of either of these options, you will find help on pages 154 and 156.

Birgit: a poem

If you were to tell part of Birgit's story in the form of a poem, how would you do it?

Would Birgit have said similar things to the athlete in hospital or do you think her views would have been very different?

EXTENSIONS

1 Mick Gowar describes an athlete from a poet's point of view. See if you can prepare a newspaper article that looks at the career and the current health of the same athlete.

   You may need to invent details that are not provided by the poet. These might include: name, age, sport, achievements, name of hospital.

2 How would you attempt to discourage the misuse of drugs amongst sports people?

   Plan an advertisement that might be put on the walls of changing rooms at sporting events. This could be in the form of a single poster or a series that would be used over the course of a season. Alternatively, it might be a single-sided leaflet: try to limit yourself to 100 words.

A DOG IS FOR LIFE

...not just for Christmas

That's the well known slogan coined by the National Canine Defence League (sometimes, known for short, as the NCDL) as part of their campaign to see that every dog in Britain is both wanted and well cared for.

This unit lets you discover something about this charity, how they publicise their work and seek support. In particular, it looks at how they are trying to re-home dogs which are brought into their care.

Listen to the interview with Ceris Price from NCDL in which she talks about some of their work and the issues raised by it.

The facts about the NCDL

- Established in 1891.
- The largest dog rescue charity in the UK.
- Thirteen rescue centres nationwide.
- Main work: rescue, rehabilitation and rehoming of stray, abandoned and abused dogs.

- No healthy dog is ever destroyed.
- Campaigns for welfare of dogs.
- Educates dog owners on responsible care for their pet.

FACT
There are five hundred thousand strays on the streets at any one time.

143 DOGS REPRESENTING LONG TERM AND SPONSORED DOGS (2%)
181 PUT TO SLEEP OR DIED (2.6%)
1123 CLAIMED (16.4%)
5433 REHOMED (79%)

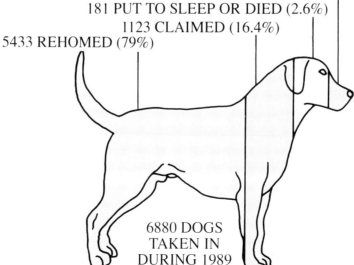

6880 DOGS TAKEN IN DURING 1989

FACT
Only one in three puppies born is actually wanted.

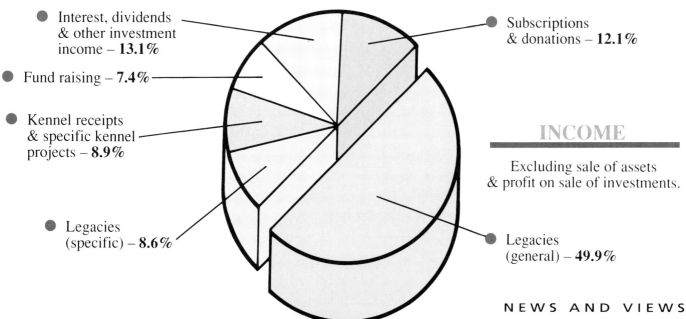

" At any one time the National Canine Defence League has over two thousand dogs in its care: some of them have been abused, some of them are strays, some of them have been abandoned, some have been handed over by their owners because they simply cannot care for them any more. Our main aim is to rehome those dogs. We do not destroy any healthy dog, and we intend to continue with that policy but that does mean that our kennels are constantly full and that we have to work very hard to find homes for dogs of whatever age, size, breed that come into our kennels and our care. **"**

● Interest, dividends & other investment income – **13.1%**

● Fund raising – **7.4%**

● Kennel receipts & specific kennel projects – **8.9%**

● Legacies (specific) – **8.6%**

● Subscriptions & donations – **12.1%**

INCOME

Excluding sale of assets & profit on sale of investments.

● Legacies (general) – **49.9%**

" Educating for more responsible dog ownership. "

" Working towards a better society for dogs. "

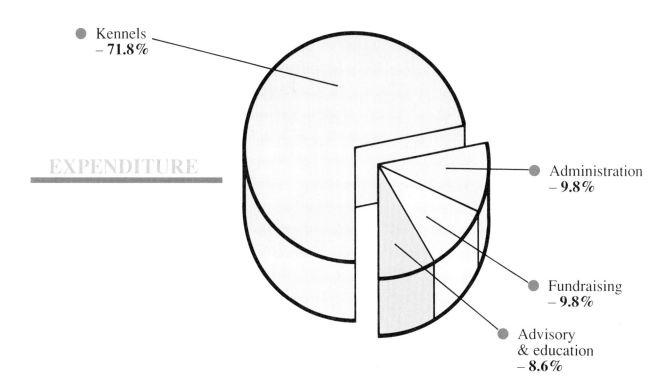

EXPENDITURE

- Kennels
  – **71.8%**

- Administration
  – **9.8%**

- Fundraising
  – **9.8%**

- Advisory
  & education
  – **8.6%**

"When people come and adopt a dog from us, they don't know the history. You have got to make certain allowances for taking in a dog that has a past of perhaps abuse or several weeks on the street as a stray. The dogs might be psychologically disturbed, they might be ill, they might just be old. You have certain problems with an eight-year-old dog, for example, that you wouldn't have with a puppy. We are trying to get the public to be aware of what they are taking on with a rescue dog: how to cope with it and how to be patient.

It is like adopting a child. The difference is that your child grows older, your child gets more independent. A dog will not do that: it will always be dependent on you for vetinary care, for boarding, for love, for food, for exercise... whatever. Unfortunately, a lot of people who take dogs don't realise that."

Decisions and Design

1 Looking at these pages, what do you think the NCDL needs from the general public in the way of help and support?

2 If you were helping the NCDL, what do you think would be the strongest points of your appeal to the public in order to get their support?

3 Design a poster either to attract attention to some part of NCDL's work or to the needs of dogs generally.

In 1989 the NCDL found homes for 5433 dogs it had rescued. They decided, with good reason, that there was a need for a leaflet about how to care for a rescued dog once it was taken to its new home.

 Listen to the cassette again and decide what you think you would want to tell people who are planning to take home a dog that has previously been abandoned.

THE CARE OF YOUR RESCUE DOG

National Canine Defence League

1 Pratt Mews, London NW1 0AD
Telephone: 071-388 0137

A Rescued Dog

The leaflet that the NCDL produced had two main sections to it. The first is shown on these two pages.

THE HISTORY OF YOUR DOG

The NCDL always gather as much information about the history of a dog as possible, as well as watching him carefully whilst he is kennelled with us. It is our aim to give you as much detail about his past as we can, though in some cases the dog is handed over to us without any background, particularly if he was a stray. The history of your pet will tell you a lot about him, his personality and his behaviour. We would recommend that you pay particular attention to any of the information that our staff are able to give you as it will enable both you and your dog to understand each other better.

SOME IMPORTANT TIPS

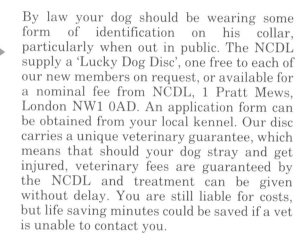

By law your dog should be wearing some form of identification on his collar, particularly when out in public. The NCDL supply a 'Lucky Dog Disc', one free to each of our new members on request, or available for a nominal fee from NCDL, 1 Pratt Mews, London NW1 0AD. An application form can be obtained from your local kennel. Our disc carries a unique veterinary guarantee, which means that should your dog stray and get injured, veterinary fees are guaranteed by the NCDL and treatment can be given without delay. You are still liable for costs, but life saving minutes could be saved if a vet is unable to contact you.

Register with a vet straight away, don't wait for an emergency.

Ensure that your dog receives a full course of vaccinations once a year. The NCDL vaccinate all the dogs at their kennels, so be sure to ask when your pet will need another course of injections. Your dog should also be wormed at least twice a year.

If your dog has not already been neutered, we strongly recommend that you have this done as soon as possible. Your vet will advise you as to the best time.

Your dog should have a bed of his own, so that he can get away from the family should he feel the need. It will also provide him with a spot in which he feels secure – especially during the first few days or weeks.

Feed your pet at regular times and don't feed him tit-bits between meals. Also ensure that he has his own bowls and cutlery. These should be kept apart from those used by your family and should be washed separately.

Keep your dog on a lead whenever you are in a public place or near farm animals.

Do not allow your pet to foul buildings, pavements, lawns or areas where children play. Train him to defecate in the gutter and carry a scoop or plastic bags with you so that you can clean up after him.

Do not allow your dog to be noisy and disturb your neighbours.

Never take him into food shops.

When you book your holiday remember your dog. Boarding kennels need to be booked early, particularly if you are going on holiday during peak time. Contact the NCDL and find out about their boarding facilities.

Train your dog to be obedient. If you have no experience of training go to your local Dog Training Club. Your vet, library or local paper will be able to give you a contact phone number.

Cassette and Leaflet

1 Ceris Price, in the interview, said that adopting a dog is a lot like adopting or looking after a young child. What can you see in these guidelines which confirms that view?

2 What differences can you see between the cassette and the leaflet? What are the advantages and disadvantages of each of these ways of communicating?

Male or Female

The NCDL has decided in this leaflet to refer to the rescued dogs as him. This is not because they only help male dogs but thay have chosen this way of writing.
Why do you think they have done this?
The alternatives would have been these:

    use she throughout
    use he/she or she/he throughout
    use he and she alternatively
    use they
    use it

Make a note of the advantages and disadvantages of each approach. Which do you prefer? Why?

Dos and Don'ts

See if you can create a list of four dos and four don'ts for an owner of a newly rescued dog.

The second section of the leaflet provides a different kind of help. Look through it and decide how you would describe this information.

A way through the detail

It can be quite difficult to remember a lot of detail all at once. See if you can pick out for a new dog owner a list of "Things to do immediately" and another of "Things to do week by week".

Make your lists short and simple enough so that they could be put up in the kitchen alongside the shopping list.

NCDL GUIDELINES FOR THE CARE OF YOUR RESCUE DOG

Firstly, we would like to thank you for offering a home to an abandoned dog from an NCDL rescue centre and we wish you many years of happiness together.

Please read the information given below carefully in preparation for settling your dog into its new home.

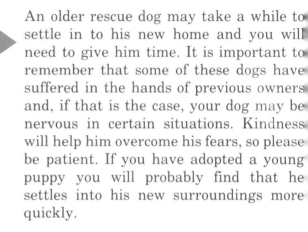 An older rescue dog may take a while to settle in to his new home and you will need to give him time. It is important to remember that some of these dogs have suffered in the hands of previous owners and, if that is the case, your dog may be nervous in certain situations. Kindness will help him overcome his fears, so please be patient. If you have adopted a young puppy you will probably find that he settles into his new surroundings more quickly.

Do not be surprised if your dog wants to be with you all the time. He may want to sleep in your bedroom with you at night. If so, start training him early by placing his own bed in your room – it is a bad idea to let him get used to sleeping on your bed.

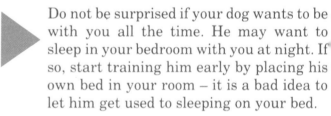 Your dog may have been kennelled for a considerable time and this is unlikely to help immediate rehabilitation, so when house training him, show him where you want him to go and be generous with your praise when he has done right. You will need to build up his confidence and trust in you.

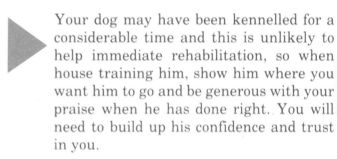 Reasons for abandonment are many, but sometimes, due to lack of love and attention, a dog may have developed some bad habits. Be firm, but kind. He needs to learn what you consider acceptable behaviour, so praise him when he has pleased you.

Although most dogs like children, please be aware that your dog may have been rejected or abandoned because he reached a stage where being pulled about by youngsters was too much for him. Educate youngsters and adults alike to treat your dog with the respect that he deserves and he will return the compliment.

We know that it is very tempting to welcome your dog by giving him a big juicy bone to chew, but please wait for a few weeks before doing this. He may guard his bone against all comers! And also remember that all bones that you give him should be large marrow bones and not one that he can splinter.

Above all, remember that patience is a virtue and that miracles do not happen overnight. Your dog is bound to be suspicious at first, and a little nervous too – as you would be in his situation. He will not understand the upheaval, so do not try to rush things. He will settle down given time.

BEAR WITH HIM, SHOW KINDNESS AND PATIENCE AND YOU WILL HAVE A FRIEND FOR LIFE.

Assignments

You have now looked at a range of information about caring for dogs.

1 Write a simple leaflet aimed at children aged 7–9 years about how they can help if their family is giving a home to an abandoned dog.

2 Write a single page leaflet that could be given out at the end of a talk about the charity at a secondary school or youth club. The Leaflet should give young people an idea of the work of NCDL as well as getting over its main concerns about the care of dogs.

BEGGARS AND CHOOSERS

The next few pages look directly at the way a newspaper presents the information it has collected. It also gives you a chance to do some reporting of your own, once you have thought about the headlines, the articles and the photographs that the newspaper chose.

What do the articles say?

Skimming: if you were reading these articles in a newspaper, you might well want to find out quickly what they say, then go back to read the parts that interest you most in more detail. Look quickly over the three articles and say what is in each of them in a single sentence. Do not worry about the detail.

Looking at the picture

1 Why do you think there are two pictures of the journalist?

2 Look at the caption to the photograph. Why is the phrase down-and-out in inverted commas?

3 Where else might you find inverted commas used like this?

4 See if you can come up with another caption for the photograph.

5 If you were the photographer what other scene might you have wanted to capture?

Expressman
Ian McKerron

A helping hand for 'down-and-out' McKerron

TRYING TO MAKE RICHES OUT OF RAGS

BEGGAR Derek Hoy boasts he can make £250 a day on the streets of London.

The £135-a-week factory worker has given up his job and now makes his living standing outside Embankment Station with a sign saying: "I'm not workshy, but I'm starving and freezing. Please help."

After a hard day's begging, he returns to his flat, changes out of his working rags into designer gear, and lives it up at expensive nightclubs.

Yesterday the Daily Express sent reporter Ian McKerron to Waterloo Station to put Hoy's claim to the test.

McKerron posed as a beggar but with one important difference — any money he collected was to be donated to a charity for the homeless, together with a substantial gift from the Express.

This is his report.

Who says you can earn a mint out of begging?

SO FELLOW Scot Derek Hoy reckons he can make a mint out of begging.

Either he is a master conman or he is living in a fantasy world.

Dressed in my best rags and armed with a sign saying: "Jobless, Homeless — Please, Please Help", I headed for Waterloo and claimed my "pitch" outside the station's East entrance.

The only offer I received was one of advice from a sober-suited City gent who suggested I might be better engaged getting off my backside and seeking gainful employment.

It was time, I decided, to adopt the direct approach.

By IAN McKERRON

My plaintive appeal of "Spare a few coppers for Christmas?" fell mainly on deaf ears.

But before long, I had received my first donation — a 50p piece from a young woman who apologised it wasn't more.

Almost magically, her kindness seemed to start a chain reaction. Ten and 20p pieces started tinkling with almost monotonous regularity in the bottom of my box.

Most donations were given without inquiry. But one elderly lady wanted to know where I was from and how I had come to be down on my luck before depositing 17p in my box and an extra strong mint in my hand.

"I should save enough to get back home to your family if I were you," she said.

"You can't do this for the rest of your life."

With darkness falling I decided to call it a day and count my takings. Three cold, degrading hours had netted the grand total of £5.68 — plus the extra strong mint.

For those who are forced to beg to survive, I have nothing but the greatest sympathy and, I have to say, some respect. Begging is a hard and humiliating way to make a living.

Dozens arrested in street

MORE than 60 people a week are arrested on the streets of London for begging, it was revealed yesterday.

The majority are homeless teenagers sleeping rough who have come to the capital attracted by the chance of a new life.

Under the 1824 Vagrancy Act it is illegal to beg for food or money.

Those arrested face a maximum fine of £400, but most are fined between £10 and £40 or jailed for a day.

According to the housing charity Crisis, many of the 4,000 homeless in London are forced to beg to stay alive.

Appeal for hospital refuges

HEALTH Secretary Kenneth Clarke is to consider opening empty hospital wards to the homeless for Christmas.

The pledge came yesterday after campaigners for single homeless in London saw Junior Health Minister Roger Freeman.

They urged him to open empty wards for those sleeping rough after four weeks of sub-zero temperatures.

The charity Single Homelessness in London claims there are at least 1,000 people sleeping on the capital's streets.

Last night a Health Department spokesman said: "Mr Clarke will be informed and action considered to see if it is appropriate or feasible."

Representatives of all political parties, churches and voluntary bodies in London met the Minister to discuss the plight of the homeless yesterday.

TRYING TO MAKE RICHES OUT OF RAGS

BEGGAR Derek Hoy boasts he can make £250 a day on the streets of London.

The £135-a-week factory worker has given up his job and now makes his living standing outside Embankment Station with a sign saying: "I'm not workshy, but I'm starving and freezing. Please help."

After a hard day's begging, he returns to his flat, changes out of his working rags into designer gear, and lives it up at expensive nightclubs.

Yesterday the Daily Express sent reporter Ian McKerron to Waterloo Station to put Hoy's claim to the test.

McKerron posed as a beggar but with one important difference — any money he collected was to be donated to a charity for the homeless, together with a substantial gift from the Express.

This is his report.

The opening article

If you are looking down the page of the newpaper this is the first part you come to.

1 Can you see any ways in which the title or the opening attempt to grab our attention?

2 Looking back at the whole of this article, what do you think is its purpose?

The main headline

1 How do you think you would say this question if you were speaking aloud?

2 What tone would you use?

3 Why do you think the word mint was chosen for the headline?

Who says you can earn a mint out of begging?

The main article

1 How does the tone of this opening compare with the headline?

2 Why do you think the second sentence is in italics?

SO FELLOW Scot Derek Hoy reckons he can make a mint out of begging.

Either he is a master conman or he is living in a fantasy world.

Dressed in my best rags and armed with a sign saying: "Jobless, Homeless — Please, Please 'Help", I headed for Waterloo and claimed my "pitch" outside the station's East entrance.

The only offer I received was one of advice from a sober-suited City gent who suggested I might be better engaged getting off my backside and seeking gainful employment.

It was time, I decided, to adopt the direct approach.

My plaintive appeal of "Spare a few coppers for Christmas?" fell mainly on deaf ears.

But before long, I had received my first donation — a 50p piece from a young woman who apologised it wasn't more.

Almost magically, her kindness seemed to start a chain reaction. Ten and 20p pieces started tinkling with almost monotonous regularity in the bottom of my box.

Most donations were given without inquiry. But one elderly lady wanted to know where I was from and how I had come to be down on my luck before depositing 17p in my box and an extra strong mint in my hand.

"I should save enough to get back home to your family if I were you," she said.

"You can't do this for the rest of your life."

With darkness falling I decided to call it a day and count my takings. Three cold, degrading hours had netted the grand total of £5.68 — plus the extra strong mint.

For those who are forced to beg to survive, I have nothing but the greatest sympathy and, I have to say, some respect. Begging is a hard and humiliating way to make a living.

The old lady

The story of the elderly lady takes up more space than any other single part of the main article. Look at it and decide why Ian McKerron focused on her.

> Most donations were given without inquiry. But one elderly lady wanted to know where I was from and how I had come to be down on my luck before depositing 17p in my box and an extra strong mint in my hand.
>
> "I should save enough to get back home to your family if I were you," she said.
>
> "You can't do this for the rest of your life."

The subsidiary articles

1 Two smaller pieces are linked with the main article. What do each of these pieces add to our understanding of beggars and begging?

2 If you had to remove one of these articles because of a shortage of space, which one would you cut out? Why?

Dozens arrested in street

MORE than 60 people a week are arrested on the streets of London for begging, it was revealed yesterday.

The majority are homeless teenagers sleeping rough who have come to the capital attracted by the chance of a new life.

Under the 1824 Vagrancy Act it is illegal to beg for food or money.

Those arrested face a maximum fine of £400, but most are fined between £10 and £40 or jailed for a day.

According to the housing charity Crisis, many of the 4,000 homeless in London are forced to beg to stay alive.

The paragraphs

Look at the length of the paragraphs. If you compare them with the paragraphs of nearly all books, you will find these newspaper paragraphs are much shorter. Why do you think this might be?

Appeal for hospital refuges

HEALTH Secretary Kenneth Clarke is to consider opening empty hospital wards to the homeless for Christmas.

The pledge came yesterday after campaigners for single homeless in London saw Junior Health Minister Roger Freeman.

They urged him to open empty wards for those sleeping rough after four weeks of sub-zero temperatures.

The charity Single Homelessness in London claims there are at least 1,000 people sleeping on the capital's streets.

Last night a Health Department spokesman said: "Mr Clarke will be informed and action considered to see if it is appropriate or feasible."

Representatives of all political parties, churches and voluntary bodies in London met the Minister to discuss the plight of the homeless yesterday.

Your own article

You have been asked by your school newspaper to produce an article on begging.

The editor has asked you to write about 300 words. She is also planning to have a picture, cartoon or diagram to accompany your piece.

You intend to do some of your own work but decide that the *Daily Express* article can provide some useful material.

The facts of the matter

As a reporter, you will want to sort out the facts.

Make a list of the facts which you think might be useful and which can be found in the newspaper articles.

Do not worry at this stage about how you will use them.

Opinions about the subject

The newspaper articles also provide some opinions and claims about begging.

Which ones do you think are important?

Make a note of two or three of them.

The *Daily Express* experiment

You will not want to go into all the details about how the *Daily Express* decided to find out about begging. However, you might decide that it was worth explaining what they did in a few sentences. Make a rough draft of that.

Your own research

There are several ways in which you might find material on this subject:

1 Library resources

You will need to think about the headings under which you might find material about begging.

Several key words can be found in the newpaper articles if you scan them carefully. A Thesaurus might also be helpful.

In the library look at the information books and at the reference section. A sheet about the way libraries are set out is available in **Heinemann English Assessment and Reference File.**

2 Opinions and stories from other people

Before you ask your friends or your family, you need to decide what questions you are going to ask. It is usually best to ask just a few questions and concentrate on getting a good variety of answers. Try to avoid questions which can be answered by yes or no.

You will also need to decide how to record your answers.

Pen and paper?

Cassette recorder?

In doing this research, you may unearth interesting stories as well as views.

People who have lived in more than one country or who have lived for a long time are often a rich source of experience and knowledge just waiting to be asked.

3 Other sources

These might include:

other newspapers

poetry/song lyrics

magazines

your own experience

your own opinions.

First Draft

One big challenge is deciding what to keep and what to throw away. Remember that it is easier to have more than 300 words and edit rather than to have fewer and have to add extra parts.

You will need to think particularly about the impression given of begging by what you choose to include.

- Are you giving a very negative view in which beggars are seen as lazy and good for nothing?

- Are you giving a very positive view which encourages the reader to view beggars with great sympathy?

- Are you attempting to express a variety of opinions and let the reader decide?

> **NEWSPAPER STYLES**
> There are other newspaper/magazine articles for you to look at to get a sense of the possible styles on pages 48 and 100.

Re-drafting

Before you write a second draft of your article, look through it with these points in mind.

- Do the paragraphs link together sensibly?
- Have I got the paragraphs in the best order?
- Is my meaning clear?
- Does it sound right or do I need to change any words/phrases?
- Is the spelling and punctuation accurate?
- Has anything important been missed out?

Second Draft

Once you have made the neccessary changes and corrections, set out your second draft so that it looks as much like a newspaper article as possible.

Another important challenge is to make your writing sound like a newspaper article. One important aspect of newspaper writing is that 'I' and 'we' are often dropped in favour of less personal phrases.

For example:

I think that....

It became clear that....

Keeping the writing brief and to the point is also important. Remember as well that newspaper paragraphs are usually shorter than normal ones.

When you have finished, see if you can come up with a suitable headline.

FREE AT LAST

Every day, important events happening all around the world are brought into our homes through the media of television and radio.

We take this almost instantaneous reporting of world affairs very much for granted, and would generally fail to notice if different news programmes presented the same items of news in significantly different ways. Or would we?

Here are three different news reports of the same event - the release of Nelson Mandela after 27 years' imprisonment for his fight against apartheid in South Africa. Two are taken from television news broadcasts: Newsround (BBC's news bulletin for young people) and the main ITN news at 5:40 pm. The third report is from the BBC radio news at 5:00 pm.

report 1

Mr Nelson Mandela on his first full day of freedom for 27 years has been talking about the future of South Africa. Speaking at a news conference in Cape Town he said that he was committed to peace but he understood the apprehension of the country's whites.

Mr Mandela has now arrived on the outskirts of Johannesburg, from where he is expected to travel to his home in the nearby township of Soweto.

Earlier, about 50 people were injured at a sports stadium where thousands had gathered to welcome him. They were crushed when a section of terrace collapsed.

... Nelson Mandela held a news conference this morning before leaving Cape Town for Johannesburg, after yesterday's jubilant but also sometimes violent scenes surrounding his release.

The setting for the news conference could hardly have been more of a contrast, the lawn, in front of Archbishop Desmond Tutu's imposing residence, in a white suburb of Cape Town.

Mr Mandela, as assured as if he had been holding news conferences for the past 27 years, instead of languishing in prison, fielded questions about white fears, the ANC's use of violence and the prospects for negotiation. And he said that he wanted to step once again on the stones he stepped on as a child in Transkei.

Southern Africa correspondent Michael Wooldridge was there ...

Soweto's huge, chaotic welcome as they await Mandela's return home. He says official talks about the future will begin soon.

Good evening, Nelson Mandela has just arrived back in Johannesburg a few miles from his home in Soweto. Tens of thousands of cheering supporters have packed a Soweto football ground all day, hoping to welcome the black nationalist leader. Dozens collapsed in the heat and the crush.

... It was a day which began with high hopes and almost ended in tragedy. From all over the township people converged on the Orlando stadium, expecting to hear Nelson Mandela. The stadium has a capacity for 50,000 people; there were many more than that here today, clinging anywhere they could for a vantage point. The crush of those coming down this funnel pressed others onto the gates against the ground. The gates were

opened slightly to allow the injured to be passed over the heads of the crowd. The worst was only avoided by opening the gates completely, allowing the crowd onto the ground. But there were several injuries. And the sun took its toll during the long wait, while Nelson Mandela and his advisers met in Cape Town to ponder the consequences of disappointing the people of Soweto.

The spring had gone from their step as they went home disappointed, a marked contrast to the way they came this morning...

... Edward Sturton, Soweto.

In South Africa, Nelson Mandela, a free man, returns home. But people are injured in the crush to greet him.

Hello again, and there's just one story dominating the news today. It's been the first full day of freedom for Nelson Mandela. The man, who until yesterday, was probably the world's most famous prisoner.

27 years ago he was jailed for life because of his fight against Apartheid in South Africa. He is now on his way home, a free man. And tens of thousands have turned out to greet him.

But as they packed into a local football stadium in the black township of Soweto, just outside Johannesburg, many were overcome by the heat and the crush. Six people had to go to hospital.

Mr Mandela's day began at the home of his friend, Archbishop Desmond Tutu, in Cape Town. After a stroll with his wife Winnie, he held a news conference. He said that things had changed a great

deal in South Africa since he went to jail. Now he thought that more white people seemed to support his cause.

This morning he decided not to go straight home to Soweto. But even so, tens of thousands went to the local football stadium to wait for him. And as the crowds built up so did the crush inside. Finally, the gates had to be smashed open to let people escape onto the pitch. When he heard about the crush, Nelson Mandela decided to go to Soweto after all.

The reason Nelson Mandela's freedom is so important is that it marks a big change in the way the South African Government sees the future. For years South Africa's 25 million black, Asian and mixed race people have lived under a political system which treats them as second class citizens.

Whose News?

Working in small groups, take turns to read each of the bulletins as you think they would have been read when first broadcast.

1   By considering the language of each piece carefully, can you identify the report aimed at young people, the Newsround piece?

    List as many reasons as you can for choosing this particular report.

2   Similarly, which report do you think was taken from the early evening television news of ITV?

    Again, list as many reasons for your choices as you can.

    If you can spot any differences in emphasis between these two television reports, say what this might be.

3   Finally, which report did you select as being the radio news extract? Why did you think this piece was more suited to a radio bulletin?

4   Look back again at all three reports. Then decide:

a) Which bulletin gave you the most factual information on the events surrounding the release?

b) Which bulletin gave you the least factual information?

c) Which bulletin best captured the atmosphere of the events?

Reporters, Readers, Listeners and Viewers

Busy reporters often have to rewrite their reports to suit the different news requirements of newspapers, television or radio.

1   Start by listing two or three things which are special to:

    ● spoken reports for radio

    ● spoken commentaries alongside filmed images for television

    ● written reports in newspapers.

2   Then put yourself in the place of a reporter having to cover an event.

3   The event could be one of the following:

    ● an environmental issue, such as oil spillage, acid rain etc.

    ● a major sporting event

    ● the birth of triplets or another "human interest" story

    ● a political demonstration, local or national.

4   Write out three versions of the same report, with one version as a short item on a Radio One news bulletin, another for an article in a popular newspaper, and the third aimed at the Six O'Clock News on the BBC.

a) Think carefully about the type of audience that would be listening, reading or viewing your report.

b) Consider the language you are using: its difficulty; how it might link with pictures; how it might create atmosphere.

c) How much background information do you need to give? How much can you assume is already there?

    Use the different strengths of each of the three media to make your report as interesting and appealing as you can.

5   When you have completed your reports, read them through and discuss them in small groups. Decide which report works best, in which medium, and for what reasons.

UNQUALIFIED

At the end of eleven years' schooling, many pupils leave with a positive pile of qualifications. In most schools, very few pupils leave with a qualification in parenthood. Perhaps that is one reason why magazines are full of problem pages with letters that include difficulties at home. This unit looks at some of the problems that parents and their children face and gives you the chance to offer some solutions. But, be warned. If you are tempted to be unsympathetic, in twenty years' time, your sons or daughters may be writing to the magazines about you!

Dear Janice
Your problems answered . . .

Gambling mum's money

I don't know if you can help but I think I've got a problem. Since last year I've been taking the odd 50p from my mum's purse when she wasn't looking and picking up change left around the home. I've been using it to play a fruit machine at the local arcade. I have already spent my £3 pocket money on it. Should I own up to her?

Susan, aged 15

* Your best tactic for the moment is to stop taking money from your mum and at the same time ask her advice about fruit machines.

She may already be wondering why you don't seem to be buying anything with your pocket money.

When you feel ready, tell your mum about the stolen money, she may understand and forgive you. That way you will not be forever carrying around your guilty secret.

Fruit machines are big business and you will never win more than you put in. The machines are programmed for you to lose. People of all ages are fighting this form of addiction.

Before you feel the urge to play, imagine the company raking in the profit from your pocket, then think of other things you could do with it instead.

I hate my life

Please help me. My teachers are always on at me to do better at school and my best friend never has time for me now she's found a boyfriend. I also feel tired all the time and have to be dragged from my bed in the mornings by my mother, who never stops moaning at me. I just wish I could go to sleep and never wake up. I hate my life. I cry a lot and can't seem to control my moods. Why do I feel like this? No-one seems to understand.

Lorna, aged 14

Secretive smoking mum

I have a problem I need some advice with; well, not really my problem - my mum's. Ever since she and my dad divorced seven years ago she has been smoking. At first it was quite plain and she smoked in public, but after a couple of years she stopped. At least I thought she stopped. I found out that she still smoked when she was on her own and in the toilet. I tried to convince her to stop and she did for a while, but now she has begun again. Do I confront her?

Chris, aged 13

Bedtime blues

A boy aged nine wrote to you and complained that he had to go to bed at nine o' clock. I am 14 and I have to go to bed at nine o' clock! During term time my mother tells me to go to bed early just because she wants to get me out of the way. My younger brother Paul is 11 and he gets to stay up until I go to bed. When I was his age I had to go to bed at eight o'clock. My brother always comes first, especially in my dad's books. My oldest sister says that I'll just have to live with it. What can I do? I am desperate. My parents are driving me around the bend.

Wendy, aged 14

* You think your parents are being unfair and inconsistent. In their eyes they are probably desperate for some peace at the end of the day. Do you nag and whinge?

The only way to change the situation is to negotiate with your mother or father. Explain that in your view they have changed the rules in Paul's favour and that you would like the differentials reinstated. In normal English, it's not fair and can you please go to bed later.

But be careful, maybe they will say Paul has to go to bed earlier and your bedtime will stay the same.

Getting away

I am very ashamed of my problem. I am 15 and cannot go away from home for more than one night without getting very, very homesick.
When someone asks me to go and stay with them overnight I make excuses that we are going away. I have talked to my family but they just say I am a baby.
I am getting very worried about this problem.

Sally, aged 15

Discussion Points

What sort of advice would you give in each of these situations?

How would you attempt to explain the parents' behaviour in each of these cases?

What do you think would be the most effective responses in these situations?

Answering a problem

You are a junior reporter on *Nooz*, the young people's paper that runs the problem page on which these letters will appear. Your boss has completed two of the replies but has gone to Spain for ten days leaving you to finish the answers. See if you can offer some straightforward, sensible and sympathetic advice.

Parenting can be done by anyone - it's not only mothers and fathers who bring up a family - grandparents, foster parents, uncles, aunts, elder brothers and sisters may all have a role.

Comparing the way I've been brought up and the way my brothers/sisters have been brought up.

Everything that parents ought to know but their sons and daughters never tell them.

Comparing the way my parents have treated me with the way my friends' parents have treated them.

Good/bad things about the way my parents have brought me up.

In Britain about one in three marriages end in divorce. In the United States, it is even higher: one in two marriages.

What did your grandparents teach your parents before/after they got married about bringing up a family?

The rules in our house: fair or unfair?

Comparing this generation with previous generations, are the stories which start "When I was your age ..." ever true?

What about a training course before couples are allowed to have babies?

Do schools miss out important matters like "how to be a parent" in the chase for more and more qualifications?

Parents: the people in this world who are least qualified for the job they do.

Writing about Parents

Most young people moan about parents now and then but serious discussion about how parents do their job is relatively rare.

It seems a bit unfair to complain about parents without looking at the problems parents face logically and reasonably.

See if you can write a young person's view of parenting that would be useful to families who have young babies but have yet to face the problems of those babies growing up!

In this first stage of the writing there are no rules and no limits about what you can write.

You can write mainly or entirely about your own family. You can choose not to write about your family at all and write instead about what you see around you in the lives of others. You can write about your family and about others.

You can choose to follow up as many or as few of the ideas, thoughts, facts and questions on this page as you wish.

The important thing at this stage is that you get down as much material as you can.

Reviewing Your Material

Once you have a good collection of material, you can put it aside and relax ...

... but not for too long because you've got to decide how to get the best out of what you have written.

Don't make any major changes to the material at this stage but make notes in the margin about the things you might want to change.

You also need to be thinking about how you organise your material.

Here are some of the things you might think about:

- are any parts of my work long-winded?
- do I repeat myself?
- which parts are not very clear and may need to be rewritten?
- is there a strong section which I might use at the beginning?
- which part sums up best how I feel and might be used at the end of the finished piece?
- do any sections need to be removed altogether because they are weak?

In Pairs

Once you have reviewed your own work, it is important to test your feelings about it against someone else's reactions.

1 Read each other's work and make notes in the same way as you did about your own writing.

2 Check punctuation and spelling.

3 When you have both finished, compare notes.

4 Where you agree a change is necessary, make it.

5 Where you disagree, talk about it and see if you can decide what is the best response.

Sometimes it helps to get a third person to read the part about which you have disagreed.

It can also help to read work aloud in order to hear what it sounds like.

EXTENSION

Write a series of short rules or short pieces of advice for new parents. For example:

1 Don't say "no" when you mean "maybe".

2 If you expect your daughter to help with the washing up, you should expect your son to help with the washing up.

The Finishing Touches

Now you are ready to make the necessary changes to your writing and to put it into the best order. This is often the best time to write your opening or closing paragraph.

NOT FAIR

EXTENDED WORK ON A THEME

"It's not fair," is something that almost everyone has said at one time or another. Sometimes the complaint is painfully true. Many people do not get the chances we might think that they are entitled to. At other times, the complaint is no more than a moan, often from someone who is lazy or who doesn't realise how lucky they are.

In this section you will be looking at several different situations involving ideas about fairness. It is important that you should feel free to express your opinion, even if you are the only person who thinks that way. It is also important that you should listen with an open mind to what other people have to say. Sometimes you may end up with a very definite view and at other times you may feel that two or three views are equally reasonable. Whatever you write, try to make it as clear and as enjoyable as possible. This will be helped by good planning and by careful re-drafting where necessary.

At the end of this section is a group of ideas for writing called **Extensions**. If you happen to be a quick worker you may get a chance to do one or several of these. You may find yourself with a free choice in **Extensions** or your teacher may direct you to one of them in order to achieve a balance with some of the work you have already done.

Getting away with it

When you are reading this story, try to imagine how it might feel to be one of the characters. Think about what your attitude might be and how you would explain your views if you were challenged.

The characters are:

Gogi - who tells the story
Linda - her sister
Dorine - her stepmother
Big Red - Dorine's friend
Gogi's father

She

"Just where do you think you're going?" she said.

"To the bathroom," I said.

"No you're not," she said, "not before you wash up these dishes."

"This is a matter of urgent necessity," I said. I hated that even my going to the bathroom had to be questioned.

"Don't want to hear," she said. "I'm sick and tired of emergency, emergency every night after dinner. Get to that sink."

"I'll wash the dishes," Linda said. She got up and started to clear off the table. I slipped out of the kitchen. The angry voice followed me down the hall:

"Linda, don't keep letting your sister get away with everything."

"I don't mind - really, Dorine," Linda said.

"That girl's just too damn lazy ... ". I shut the bathroom door to muffle the sounds of her grievances against me. She didn't like me. She never had. And I didn't care. Stepmothers ...!

Searching the bottom of the hamper for the science fiction magazine I had hidden beneath the dirty clothes, I sat on the toilet and began to get out of this world - as far from her as I could get.

From the day she had walked into our house she'd been onto me. I was lying on my bed reading when she and Daddy pushed into my room without knocking. Our eyes locked. She didn't speak. Neither did I.

I was in a panic. Daddy had forbidden me to read fairy tales. "At twelve years old! You too old," he'd said. He wanted me to read only school books. I hadn't had time to hide the book of fairy tales beneath my mattress as I usually did. I curled up around it, praying to keep his eyes from it.

But Daddy was only showing her the apartment. So she had to turn to inspect my almost bare room. When she looked back at me, her eyes said: What are you doing reading in this miserable room instead of doing something useful around this terrible house? My eyes answered. What's it to you?

They left the room the way they'd come. Abruptly. Hearing their footsteps going towards the kitchen, I got up and followed. Linda was in the kitchen, washing fish for our dinner. When they went in, Linda looked and smiled.

"What a lovely girl," Dorine said, and the shock of her American accent went through me. What was Daddy doing with an American woman! "She's got to be the prettiest child I ever did see. My name is Dorine," she said.

From the first she had chosen Linda over me. Maybe because Linda was pretty, with her long, thick hair and clear brown eyes and brown velvet skin. I was plain-looking. Or maybe because Linda was two years older - already a teenager.

"You're Daddy's friend," Linda said, batting her long black eyelashes the way she always did whenever someone paid her a compliment. " I didn't know Daddy had a lady friend." Daddy gave Linda a quick look and she changed to: "My name is Linda. And that's" - she pointed to where I stood in the doorway - "the baby. Her name is Gogi."

But Dorine had already turned away from Linda to inspect the kitchen. And suddenly I saw our kitchen and the sweat of embarrassment almost drowned me: the sink was leaking and had a pan under it to catch the dirty water; the windowpanes were broken and stuffed with newspaper to keep out winter; the linoleum was worn, showing the soft wood beneath.

And she wore furs. Our mother had never worn furs. Not even when Daddy had had lots of money. People from the tropics didn't think of wearing things like furs. And the way Dorine looked around – nose squinched up, mouth pulled back – judging us, West Indians.

Daddy stood in the middle of the kitchen, quieter than usual - big, broad, handsome in his black overcoat, around his arm the black crepe band of mourning. His hands were deep in the pockets of his grey wool suit. And she hit out at him: "Damn, Harry, how can you live like this!"

Linda stopped smiling then. Daddy's eyebrows quivered. My mouth got tight with satisfaction. Daddy had a mean temper. I waited for him to blast her out of our house and out of our lives. She had socked us where we hurt – our pride.

"How you mean?" Daddy had said. "We ain't live so. You see mi restaurant ..." So, he had known her while our mother was still alive. "... I lose it," he said. "Mi wife dead. I sell me house, mi furniture, mi car. I-I-mi friend let me stay here for a time - but only for a short time." He was begging! I hated that he stood there begging.

"If it's only one minute, that's one minute too damn long," she said.

Lifting my head from the science fiction magazine to turn a page, I heard the sound of pots banging against pans in the kitchen. And I heard Dorine's footsteps in the hall. I waited for the knob to turn on the bathroom door. She sometimes did that. But this time she went on into the living room. A short time later I heard the television playing.

It had been two years since the pointing, the ordering, the arranging and rearranging of our lives had begun. She had forced us to leave our old free apartment and move into her big one with its big rooms, its big kitchen and all those dozens of pots and pans for all things and all occasions. We had to listen to her constant: "Cleanliness is next to godliness", and "A good housekeeper has a place for everything and keeps everything in its place". Like who told her that what we wanted most in life was to be housekeepers? I didn't!

Daddy let her get away with everything. He stayed out most days looking for work. And he spent evenings gambling with his friends. The times he spent at home he spent with her – laughing and joking in their bedroom. She entertained him to keep him there. I'd see her flashing around the house in her peach-coloured satin dressing gown, her feet pushed into peach-coloured frilly mules, her big white teeth showing all across her face, her gown falling away to expose plump brown knees. Guess that's what he liked – that combination of peach satin and smooth brown skin.

She worked, a singer. Sometimes for weeks she'd be out on the road. Then she'd come home with her friends and they'd do all that loud American talking and laughing. She sometimes brought us lovely things back from "the road". Blouses, underwear, coats. She won Linda's affection like that and might have won mine if I hadn't heard a man friend say to her one day: "Dorine, it's bad enough you got yourself hooked up with that West Indian. But how did you manage to get in a family way?"

"Big Red," she called him. "I'm in love."

"With all of 'em?" he asked.

"They come with the deal," she said.

"Some deal," he answered.

"You don't need to worry none, Big Red," she said. "They earn their keep."

She saw me standing in the doorway then, and her big eyes stretched out almost to where I stood. Guilty. Her mouth opened. I walked away. I had heard enough. I went right in and told Linda. "That's what she wants us around for," I said. "To be her maids."

"Gogi," Linda said. "She probably didn't mean it that way at all."

"What other way could she mean it?" I asked. Innocent Linda. She never saw the evil in the hearts and minds of people.

But from that day Dorine picked on me. When I vacuumed the hall, she called me to show me specks I could hardly see and made me vacuum over again. When I cleaned my room, she went in and ran her fingers over the woodwork to show me how much dust I had left behind. "That ain't the way we do things around here," she liked to say. "Do it right or don't do it at all." As though I had a choice!

"Trying to work me to death, that's what she's doing," I complained to Linda.

"But why don't you do things right the first time, Gogi?" Linda said. I could only stare at her. My sister!

We had always been close. Linda hadn't minded doing things for me before Dorine came, as long as I read to her. Linda never had time for things like reading. She knew she was pretty and kept trying to make herself perfect. Linda washed her blouses and underwear by hand. She ironed her clothes to defeat even the thought of a wrinkle. And she had always done mine along with hers, just to have me read to her.

But now our stepmother who had turned our father against us had turned my sister against me! Well, if Linda wanted to be a maid, that was her business. I did enough when I vacuumed the hall and cleaned my room. If Linda had to take Dorine's side against me, then let Dorine read for her. I was satisfied to do my reading to myself - by myself.

Sitting too long on the toilet, I felt the seat cut into my thighs. I got up to unstick myself and leaving the toilet unflushed – not to give away that I had finished – I sat on the closed stool, listening to what ought to have been sounds of glass clinking against glass, of china against china.

The quiet outside the bathroom unsettled me. I usually knew when Linda had finished with the dishes. I always heard when she passed to join Dorine in the living room. They played the television loud, thinking to make me jealous, making me feel unneeded, pretending not to care that I had shut myself from them and that I might go to my room without even a goodnight. But I hadn't heard Linda pass!

The television kept playing. I strained to hear the programme to tell the time. It was on too low. Getting up, I thought of going out to see how things were but sat down again. Better to give Linda a little more time. I started another story.

I had only half finished when my concentration snapped. The television had been turned off. I tried to but couldn't get back into the story. Instead I sat listening, hoping to pick up sounds from the silent house. What time was it?

Getting up, I put my ear to the door. No outside sound. Unlocking the door, I cracked it open and peeked out. The hallway was dark! Everybody had gone to bed! How late was it? Taking off my shoes I started tiptoeing down towards my room. Then from the dark behind me I heard: "Ain't no sense in all that creeping. Them dishes waiting ain't got no ears." I spun around. A light went on and there she was, lying on a chaise longue that had been pulled up to the living room door. "That's right, it's me," she said. "And it's one o'clock in the morning. Which gives you enough time to wash every dish in the sink squeaking clean before one o'clock noon."

Tears popped to my eyes as she marched me down past my room, past the room where Linda slept, into the kitchen. Tears kept washing my cheeks as I washed dishes. She sat inspecting every one, acting as though we were playing games. If we were, I expected it to go on forever. She had tricked me – and she had won.

Rosa Guy

How accurate? ... opinions about the story

"I don't think Dorine's all that bad. Gogi is just lazy."

"Gogi takes after her father."

"The story is really about the price of love. Nothing comes free."

"I think the problem is that Gogi and Dorine are too much alike."

How far do you think that these opinions about the story are true?

See if you can rank them on this scale:

1	entirely true
2	mainly true
3	fairly true
4	slightly true
5	not true at all

As a group, try to come to a unanimous agreement as to how true you think each of these statements is. As you may be asked to report back, decide what you might say in order to defend your decisions.

The story is about ...

prejudice prejudice

... prejudice

What do you feel are the main prejudices that stand out in Rosa Guy's story?

What do you think of them?

How do they compare with your experience?

... justice

There are always problems when people are treated unfairly and this story is no exception.

What strikes you as the most unfair part of what happens in this story?

What other things seem unfair to you?

... language

Think about the way that Gogi's father talks, compared with the way that Gogi's stepmother talks.

How would you link the differences in the way they talk to how people behave in this story?

Another point of view

Gogi has had an opportunity to tell the story from her point of view.

How do you think the other characters might describe the family situation and especially Gogi's part in it. Choose one of them and write about the family from his or her point of view, starting on the same evening as Gogi's story.

NO IDEA

Scene   Evening. The Barrett's kitchen. It has a back door and a hallway leading off.

(Grandad enters by the back door. He wears slippers and limps heavily. He gives a disgruntled snort as he surveys the breakfast dishes on the kitchen table.
He sits and begins to read a newspaper. We hear the front door open and shut. Grandad doesn't look up. Sandy enters and he pointedly continues reading.)

SANDY: Hi, Grandad.

GRANDAD: Oh, it's you. Where's your mother and father?

SANDY: Still at the cafe. It's been murder. On the go all day.

GRANDAD (*sour*): That makes a change.

SANDY (*Taking off coat*): Here, I saw you out back talking to old Miss Hemsley.

GRANDAD: Been on a march, she had, to the Houses of Parliament.

SANDY: Miss Hemsley!

GRANDAD: 'Fighting for our rights, Mr Barrett,' she said. 'Rights for over-sixties.'

SANDY: What'd she do? Burn her bra or summat?

GRANDAD: No respect have you?

SANDY: I think she fancies you. Last chance to get hitched before she snuffs it.

GRANDAD: There's a tamer laid up for you, young lady.

SANDY: So you keep saying. I'm going to the front room. It's time for my series.

GRANDAD: You can't watch that.

SANDY: You're not going to bed already! I suppose I could move the telly in here, into the kitchen.

GRANDAD: I'm not going to bed, I'm watching snooker.

SANDY: But it's my series!

GRANDAD: You've got your whole life to be watching these series of yours.

SANDY: But Grandad, I told you this morning I wanted to watch it.

GRANDAD: And I'm telling you I'm watching snooker. I'm entitled to watch a bit of telly at my age. Not much to ask.

SANDY: I come back specially to watch it. It's not fair.

GRANDAD: Instead of watching telly, you should be giving your mother a hand, get that washing up done. It's been there since breakfast. I don't know what sort of house this is.

SANDY: I've been working at the cafe since eight this morning. So's Mum and Dad.

GRANDAD: You don't know what work is, lass. (*Going*) Young people, you've no idea.

from **The End of the Road** *by Kara May*

Thinking about the dialogue

What is there in what Sandy says that might be expected to offend Grandad?

What is there in what Grandad says or does that might be expected to anger Sandy?

Who is being unfair?

Thinking about a performance

Quite a lot has happened at the opening of this scene before a word is said.

Read the opening stage directions again so that you have a picture in your mind of how this scene begins.

Apart from these opening directions, most of the interpretation is left to the actors. If you were directing this scene, what would you have to say about how it could best be performed? You will need to think about:

● the right tone of voice for particular speeches

● the gestures that might accompany the words

● the movements of the characters on the stage.

TEACHER'S PACK

A photocopiable version of this scene for making director's notes on is available in **Heinemann English Teacher's Pack 3**.

Describing each other

At the end of this scene Mrs Barrett and her husband have not yet arrived home from work. What do you think that Sandy might say to her mum about Grandad when she does eventually arrive? What do you think that Grandad might say about her?

Write two short scenes, the first between Sandy and Mrs Barrett, the second between Grandad and Mrs Barrett. It may help your writing to know that Grandad has been staying at the Barrett's because he has been unwell.

Use the extract from the play as a model for your own layout and presentation.

Sharks in raincoats

Geoff Howard is the vicar of a parish in Salford. Here he describes how he discovered at first hand what it is to be desperate for money and in the clutches of sharks in raincoats.

The phone rang; I dropped my fork on the plate. Another meal disturbed. It was the neighbouring vicar. Parishioners of *mine*, Marty and Pat Brown, had asked *him* for food.

I half-filled a carrier bag with groceries and set off to locate their flat. The front door of the shared entrance had been ripped off, the stair light smashed, and the steel handrail torn from the concrete steps. Their flat was devoid of luxury except for a portable 'colour' television (the picture was purple). It was being watched by seven year old Tracey, while their baby played in his cot. There were no carpets or rugs and their settee and chairs were ready for burning. There was not an ornament in the flat, no plants, not even a Christmas card. Apart from a change of underwear, their clothes were what they were wearing. Marty took off his shoes and poked a finger through the sole. Pat's shoes were cast-offs with four inch heels. They slept under blankets without sheets. The last of their food - potatoes and cabbage - was boiling on the stove. Cupboards and drawers were bare. Christmas was two days away and they had spent the last of their money on a gift for Tracey which she had already been given.

On the mantelpiece was threat of eviction, a disconnection notice from the Gas Board, and details of the £400 they owed to a loan company.

Their troubles had started when two men wearing raincoats' had knocked on their door with a bundle of bank notes and asked if they needed cash. They immediately borrowed £50 agreeing to pay back £65 at five pounds a week over thirteen weeks. The following week the men loaned them another fifty pounds. They were then repaying almost half their weekly income at the expense of paying rent and fuel bills. Whenever they found it difficult to repay the loans, they were offered more loans as a way out. When there was £45 left to pay on one card and £40 on the other, they were given two new loans of £50 to enable them to clear the debt. They were given £100 with one hand and had £85 taken back with the other. They had gained £15 in immediate cash but now owed £65 on each card.

I held the hat out for them both locally and nationally until, four weeks later, all the debts were cleared. I paid off the sharks on condition that they would never approach Marty and Pat again. They were back at Marty's door the next week. Pat and Marty were not bad people - just hopeless with money. By last December I hadn't heard from them for a couple of years, so I called on them, eleven years to the day after I had first met them. "We've sorted ourselves out," Marty said with some

pride. There were carpets, decent furniture, ornaments, pictures, a video recorder, and a Christmas tree with presents heaped under it. Marty pushed a ten pound note in my top pocket. "Use that to help someone like you've helped me." For years we had been called fools for pouring food and money into a 'hopeless' situation. Social workers and housing managers had written them off, but our willingness to help irrespective of immediate results had paid off.

This Easter I went round to see what I could learn from them with a view to helping others with similar problems. They looked embarrassed, hedged a bit. "We didn't want you to know." Pat said. "When you're broke and someone waves twenty tenners under your nose it's impossible to refuse. We've borrowed to pay for every dammed thing in the house. Even that ten quid we gave you for the poor box was borrowed! We're in it up to our necks." Rent arrears, fuel bills, hire purchase agreements, loans and mail order arrears amounted to debts of £6,000. Agreed payments were almost twice their weekly income of £61 a week.

Loan sharks* don't bother to find out the credit-worthiness of their victims. But who are the sharks? Credit card companies can increase credit limits without written consent, and mail order firms will only refuse credit to known debtors. Watch out. They may not be wearing raincoats, but they are already waving a bunch of tenners under your nose.
'WATCH OUT'

* Loan sharks - so called because sharks have a reputation for violence and for not being too fussy about who they choose as a victim. Loan sharks lend money at enormously high rates of interest to people who cannot get money in other ways and who usually cannot really afford the loan. In most cases, what they do is legal.

About the article

Did anything surprise you about this article?

In all that happened, what angered you or saddened you?

Newspapers often add short sub-headings between paragraphs in order to make an article easier for the eye to take in. The job is one of those usually done by a sub-editor. If you were sub-editing this piece for a newspaper, where would you put in sub-headings and what would they be? Try to limit your choices to four.

Try to explain how the loan sharks work.

What are the similarities and the differences between the sharks and the credit card companies?

Presenting the article

Take a look at the use of italics in this article. Why are they used? How often? What would happen if you used them a lot more often? If you are writing rather than typing, what might you use instead of italics?

In what other ways is the article helped by the way it is presented?

A Leaflet

See if you can prepare a leaflet that uses the experiences of Marty and Pat to warn others about the dangers of credit. It needs to be short enough to be read in less than a minute but powerful enough to get the message home.

A suggested format

① A large A4 sheet of paper folded in two.

② Front cover: choose a title.

③ Inside: a main message of no more than 250 words.

- get a rough draft of what you think is worth saying
- work at getting the length about right
- decide what sub-headings you want to use
- decide how you will illustrate your article
- re-draft to get a final version

④ Back cover: a short sentence or a phrase which you believe will reinforce your message.

You do not have to use this format if you can think of an alternative that is more suitable for your ideas.

TEACHER'S PACK 3

This contains appropriate graphics with which to illustrate the leaflet.

EXTENSIONS

Looking overall

1 Sympathy

a) Of all the people, real and fictional, for whom do you feel most sympathy?

b) How would you explain to a friend why the person or people you have chosen most deserve our sympathy?

2 Fact or Fiction?

a) The first two pieces you looked at were fiction and the third was a factual report. All three might be described as true to life.

b) What differences can you see between the factual and the fictional?

c) What are the advantages in each of these two ways of writing?

3 In my ideal world ...

a) What changes would you make to the world in order to make it a fairer place?

b) How would you attempt to introduce your changes?

c) Think about the issues about which you have read here but feel free to develop concerns and ideas of your own as well.

d) Think about how realistic your dreams are. What compromises might you be willing to make?

4 Story

Create a short story entitled Not Fair.

Looking at particular sections

5 Write an imagined conversation between Gogi and Linda, the two sisters in **She**, about their stepmother.

6 Look back at the extract from **The End of the Road** by Kara May. Then try to write a similar kind of scene based on the following situation:

It is a sunny afternoon in the garden. A grandson/daughter is outside reading a book and listening to music on the radio. A grandparent comes out to enjoy the sun as well and wants the radio turned off.

7 You have been offered the chance to produce a twenty second commercial for radio or television to advertise your leaflet about credit and debt. Plan and prepare your advertisement.

STORYBOARDS/TELEVISION SCRIPTS

Help with video storyboards can be found on page 158 and television script layout can be looked at on page 73.

HOT HOUSING
AND HOOLIVANS

New words are entering the language all the time. Most new words or phrases only survive for a short time but some become permanent residents. How does it happen?

(1) Some new words come from other places.

ITALY

PIZZA

ALASKA (ESKIMO)

ANORAK

ENGLISH DICTIONARY

Why do you think these words were borrowed from these places?

BARBECUE

SAUNA

CARIBBEAN

FINLAND

Can you think of any other borrowed words?

(2) Sometimes we give a word an extra role.

beaver noun

a small dam-building mammal with thick fur, webbed hind feet, a paddle-like tail and a reputation for hard work.

to beaver verb

to work hard and enthusiastically at a task

for example: She spent hours beavering away at the unfinished project.

(3) On other occasions, resident words get linked together into compound words.

green	+	house	greenhouse
go	+	get	go-getter
smoke	+	fog	smog
well	+	earned	well-earned
brain	+	wash	brainwash
butter	+	cup	buttercup

a) Check the meaning of these compound words and explain how you think they got that meaning.

b) What words do you think have been put together to make these ones?

backlash, stranglehold, motorway, sleepwalker, everywhere

c) What other compound words can you think of?

(4) Words also get shortened at times.

telephone	phone
cabriolet	cab
perambulator	pram
aeroplane	plane

a) What shortened words do we get from these?

omnibus, pianoforte, microphone, snapshots, sweetmeats

b) What other words can you think of that have been shortened in similar ways?

(5) The same word can be borrowed more than once from another language.

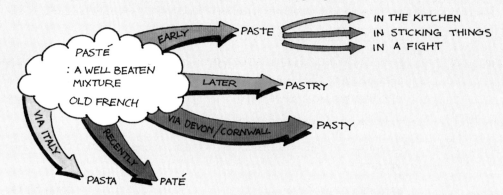

Think about the words we have created from these sources:

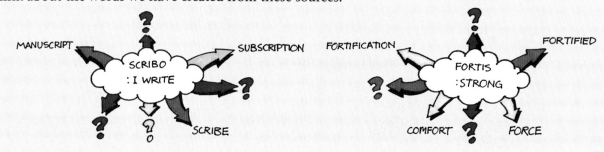

(6) Another group of words began life as someone's name.

wellington the most famous wearer of this in the early days was the Duke of Wellington.

In his day it was leather rather than rubber or plastic.

sandwich invented by John Montagu, the fourth Earl of Sandwich who wanted to keep gambling and eating at the same time. His original sandwich was filled with a large slice of beef.

leotard named after the acrobat Jules Leotard who perfected the first aerial somersault and invented the one-piece suit that still bears his name.

Heinemann Guide to New Words and Phrases

affluenza	mental illness caused by having too much money.
ambulance chaser	a person who tries to make a profit out of other people's disasters. The word was first used in the nineteenth century to describe lawyers who looked out for accident victims who could be persuaded to employ them to seek compensation.
buncing	increasing prices in order to cover loss due to shoplifting.
hoolivan	a police vehicle equipped with video for use in crowd control especially at football grounds.
hot housing	intensive teaching of young children in order to develop intelligence to a very high level.
pencil whipping	writing false certificates, for example, for repairs that have not been completed.

a) How do you think these words came about?

b) Which of these phrases, if any do you think will last? Why?

"The downside of making rockumentaries is that you can never be sure of the next job. There are no platinum handshakes in this business. Now I'm not a gloomster but if the moneymen aren't behind you, you're finished. It's no good being gobsmacked: you have to expect it."

FURTHER WORDS

downside	noun
gloomster	noun
gobsmacked	verb
moneyman	noun
platinum handshake	noun
rockumentary	noun

c) What do you think that these further words might mean? Try to explain how you reached your answers.

d) Every year produces its own crop of new ideas for words and phrases. See if you can produce a brief guide of your own. Say what the word or phrase means and, if you can, say how it came into being.

IT'S GOT TO HAVE A NAME

TELLY
My youngest brother uses this phrase. I think it's because his best friend Robert uses it and they do everything alike. Mum sometimes uses the phrase in a friendly sort of way where she's saying things like "Let's curl up in front of the telly".

THE GOGGLEBOX
It is usually Dad who calls it the gogglebox although my elder sister sometimes uses the phrase. Dad describes it like that when he thinks we've been watching far too long or we're watching a programme on a different channel from the one he wants.

TELEVISION
My elder sister calls it a television when she's dreaming about having one in her own bedroom. It makes it sound grander when she says television rather than T.V.

T.V.
The word my elder sister and my mum usually use. It sounds to me like the most normal way to describe it.

THE BOX
Dad usually calls it the box. He says that is because the first one they ever had was a twelve inch screen in a big wooden box. He claims that saying television each time would be too much of a mouthful.

WHAT'S IN A WORD?

- Why do the people mentioned here call the television by different names? What do they want to make you think of when using these words?

- What do you call a television?

- Does the word you use vary at all? If so, when and why?

- What words do your family, neighbours and friends use?

The way they say it

Chart the way that people you know say that something or someone is very good. Lay out your findings in a way that is clear and easy to follow.

Who could I ask?

members of my class

other people at school

friends

parents/grandparents

brothers/sisters

aunts/uncles

neighbours

people at youth club

Things to think about

What difference (if any) does the age of the person make to the word that gets used?

Do people use different words on different occasions? For example, do people use the same adjective to describe a car they like and a person they like?

Do any of the words you have collected sound outdated? Why do you think that might be?

WHO DO YOU THINK YOU'RE TALKING TO?

> I don't think that it matters what you say. The important thing is what you are.

> It's all very well calling him a monstink but if he doesn't know what you mean, it's not much use, is it?

Amongst the dialects in which English is spoken and written, there is one which is spoken by at least some people in nearly all parts of Britain. The national dialect - Standard English - has the great advantage of being understood by nearly all English speakers. That makes it very suitable for news broadcasts, for example, and for any situation where clear communication which can be understood by English speakers in all areas is important.

Many people use both the national dialect and their local one, depending on who they are talking to. Thomas Hardy described the situation for Mrs Durbeyfield's daughter back in 1891.

"Mrs Durbeyfield habitually spoke the dialect; her daughter, who had passed the Sixth Standard in the National School under a London-trained mistress, spoke two languages: the dialect at home, more or less; ordinary English abroad* and to persons of quality."

From **Tess of the d'Urbervilles**

* abroad = out and about

Not many people today could be described as speaking "two languages" but nearly all of us alter our speech a little to fit the circumstances.

Language for the occasion

1 Discuss what differences you think you would make to your speech if you were talking to these people.

    your favourite teacher/the headteacher

    your best friend/a newcomer to your class

    your mother/father

    your parents/grandparents

2 See if you can produce three versions of a short conversation where you try to borrow five pounds from someone. That person is not sure whether to give it to you. You want the money for a trip but you do not want to say what the trip is. Ideally you don't want to explain very much because you are embarrassed about not having the money in the first place. You don't want to make up lies but you don't want to encourage an investigation.

Version One: in the playground with a friend

Version Two: at home with a parent/other adult

Version Three: in the classroom with a teacher

You must not use any names that give away who you are speaking to or give any clues about where you are. Try to get other people to work out where you are simply by the style of the dialogue.

WOOLLY LANGUAGE

If you think learning French or Arabic or German or any other language is difficult, be sympathetic to people learning English. Because the English Language has developed from so many other languages it is unusually complicated and seems to have dozens of exceptions to even the simplest rule.

It is hardly a surprise that foreign manufacturers do not always translate their leaflets into the clearest of English. Here are the instructions that were attached to one woollen sweater.

This article was treated against the contraction it can be washed at hand and it will conserve its form and beauty if was considered next greetings.

To Wash: Invert the piece. Wash it in tepid water (40 C). Do not make white. Dissolve the detergent before the washing.

To Rinse: Employ tepid water to eliminate the residues of soap or detergent.

To Press: Press lightly without twist, or to utilise an hidro extractor. Take the shape at piece in the original dimension and dry it upon a plane area and without sun's action and highs temperatures.

To Starch: Utilise in preference to an iron of steam or to starch on a humid cloth.

Making it clear

Imagine you are the importer of these sweaters and you have the job of doing something with these instructions.

Sort out as well as you can what is meant and write it out in Standard English.

HINT

If you feel uncertain about your answer, take a look at the washing instructions on your own or your family's clothes.

Proof Reading/Drafting

Once you have achieved a set of instructions, you will need to find out if they make sense.

Working with a partner, take a good look at each other's first draft. Underline with a pencil any parts that do not seem to be clear in your partner's instructions.

When you have both done this, see if you can each produce improved versions.

Keeping It Simple

Even when you have produced a better translation of the instructions, not everyone will read them.

Manufacturers have found that the shorter and the simpler instructions are, the more likely they are to be read.

What is the briefest and simplest set of instructions you can provide for the care of this sweater?

Work with Words

To sort out these instructions, you will need to do some translating of your own.

If you are unsure about the meaning of certain words such as tepid, residues, utilise, and humid you may be helped by a dictionary.

If you want to find a word that is similar in meaning but perhaps clearer to you, you may need to turn to a thesaurus if a dictionary does not help. You can find out more about using a thesaurus in **Heinemann English Assessment and Reference File**.

WARNING

You will have to make your own mind up as to whether the writer has grasped the meaning of a word in the first place.

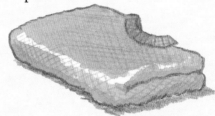

A Solution

We will probably never know quite what the original writer meant but a reasonable solution to the puzzle with which you can compare your answer is in **Heinemann English Teacher's Pack 3**.

LETTER WRITING

There are a variety of ways in which a letter can be presented. If you are uncertain about what is acceptable, ask for advice. The two most important points are that your letter needs to be clear and consistent in its presentation.

The Layout

INFORMAL

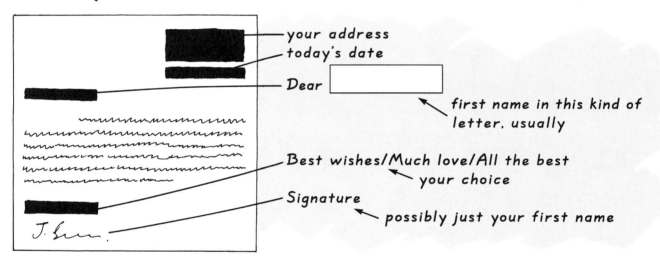

your address
today's date
Dear
first name in this kind of letter, usually
Best wishes/Much love/All the best
your choice
Signature
possibly just your first name

FORMAL

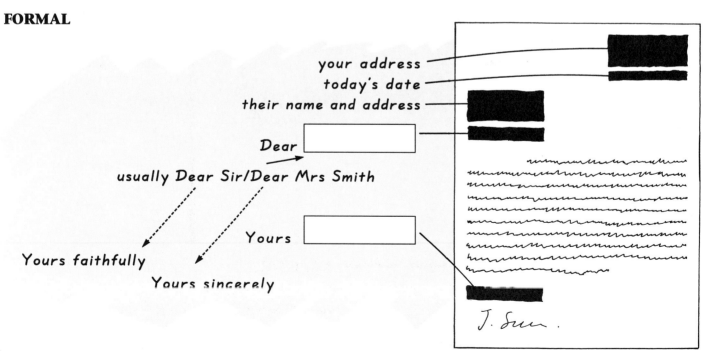

your address
today's date
their name and address
Dear
usually Dear Sir/Dear Mrs Smith
Yours faithfully
Yours sincerely
Yours

The Content of Formal Letters

76 Whiteoak Drive
Camford
Surrey DD3 9BC
23rd May 1994

The Manager
Brain Services PLC
Greystuff
Lanarkshire CS1 2OB

Dear Sir
    I wish to make arrangements to have my brain overhauled at your Skulton branch. I would be grateful if you would make an appointment for me. The easiest day for me to attend would be a Monday. My preferred method of payment is by Grabbit credit card.
    I look forward to hearing from you.
Yours faithfully

J. Silk (Mr).

if your address is not there, they cannot write back

if you say who your letter is for, it stands a better chance of landing on the right desk

REMEMBER
be polite
be clear
stick to the point

they have to be able to read your signature in order to write back

PRACTICE

Write a reply to J. Silk as if you were the manager of Brain Services PLC.

SETTING OUT

SPEECH

There are many ways of setting out what people say. One of the most commonly-used methods with our language is to use inverted commas, sometimes known as speech marks.

The two most important things to remember about them are these:

1 new speaker ... new line

2 the inverted commas go around the actual words that are spoken.

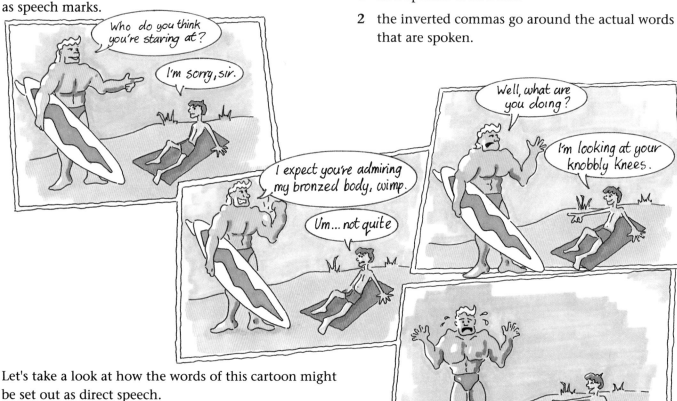

Let's take a look at how the words of this cartoon might be set out as direct speech.

The bronzed surfer was striding across the beach when he noticed a puny little newcomer looking his way.

"Who do you think you're staring at?" he demanded.

"I'm sorry, sir," the newcomer replied.

"I expect you're admiring my bronzed body, wimp," said the surfer.

The newcomer paused. "Um ... not quite."

"Well, what are you doing?"

"I'm looking at your knobbly knees."

PRACTICE

Write what you think might be the next six to eight lines of this conversation. Check your layout against the layout used here.

The detail

Inverted commas go around the words that are spoken in much the same way that bookends go around books.

Look at the way the first speech began:

The first inverted commas come right at the beginning, before the speaker starts.

The second inverted commas come right at the end of the speech, after any punctuation that is needed.

"Who . . .

. . . staring at?"

Simple guidelines for setting out speech

1   A new speaker ... a new line

2   Inverted commas enclose what is actually said

3   A new speech begins with a capital letter

4   A speech is followed by punctuation - a comma, full stop, question mark or exclamation mark.

PRACTICE

Turn the following cartoon into a story with direct speech and continue the conversation as you think it might happen.

In order to make it easy for you to look back at your punctuation, including your inverted commas, use a different colour pen to punctuate the conversation.

PLAYSCRIPT

The key to writing clear playscript is distinguishing what is said from any other information. Take a look at how this is done by printers.

GRANDAD: You don't know what work is, lass. (*Going*) Young people, you've no idea.

SANDY (*to herself*): Damn! Damn and blast!

> (*We hear the front door open and shut.*)

SANDY: That'll be Mum and Dad. I suppose I'd better get started on this.

> (*She starts washing up,* MR *and* MRS BARRETT *come into the hall.*)

MRS BARRETT: I did tell you, Eddie. Bring two pints of milk, because we've none at home.

The printers have made the characters' names stand out from what they say. They have also made the stage directions clear. This has been done by using different kinds of printing type:

italic type for the stage directions

CAPITALS FOR THE CHARACTERS' NAMES

ordinary print for what is said.

... but I'm not a printer.

When you are producing handwritten playscript the need to be clear is the same. Putting the stage directions in brackets is straightforward but you need an alternative to italics.

One solution is to underline stage directions and another is to use a different colour.

In either case it will need to be well spaced in order to be easy to follow.

> GRANDAD : You don't know what work is, lass. (Going) Young people, you've no idea.
>
> SANDY (to herself): Damn! Damn and blast!
>
> (We hear the front door open and shut.)
>
> SANDY : That'll be Mum and Dad. I suppose I'd better get started on this.
>
> (She starts washing up. MR and MRS BARRETT come into the hall.)
>
> MRS BARRETT : I did tell you, Eddie. Bring two pints of milk because we've none at home.

> GRANDAD : You don't know what work is, lass. (Going) Young people, you've got no idea.
>
> SANDY (to herself): Damn! Damn and blast!
>
> (We hear the front door open and shut)
>
> SANDY : That'll be Mum and Dad. I suppose I'd better get started on this
>
> (She starts washing up. MR and MRS BARRETT come into the hall.)
>
> MRS BARRETT : I did tell you, Eddie. Bring two pints of milk because we've none at home.

REMEMBER

When you are writing plays you are setting them out for those who will act in them for you. Think about how you would like a script to look if you were acting in someone else's play.

PRACTICE

Continue this playscript for another ten or twelve lines using one of the suggested layouts.

MAKING A
STORYBOARD

Storyboards are often used to plan film or video sequences.

The original story idea is first divided into a number of episodes or scenes, and then each scene is built up through a sequence of individual shots.

A storyboard is very useful when building up a scene, as the individual shots can be easily shown one after the other. A rough drawing of each shot allows a sequence to be visualised quickly so that changes can be made easily – adding atmosphere or giving extra story information.

Let your selection of shots tell most of the story for you. Do not worry about the technical quality of your drawing – matchstick people are fine. The important thing is to keep your storyboard visually interesting by varying your shots – going for 'close ups' in some, 'long shots' in others. Also remember to fill each frame, do not hide things away in corners or leave too much boring white space where nothing happens. (See Transport Cafe of her Nightmares on page 72 for more ideas on this. You will also find help on using storyboards in **Heinemann English Assessment and Reference File.**)

To the left of each frame, briefly describe the type of shot you are aiming at – what you want to show and how you want to show it.

To the right of each frame, write out any speech, sound effects or music you wish to include – what you need to hear and how to make it sound just right.

STORYBOARD

Complete storyboard shots 3 and 4 in this sequence. Remember to describe each shot and to write out any speech or sound effects you require.

1

Wide shot of telephone box
Set against a harsh winter scene.
Silhouette of person just visible
inside the box.

SOUND
sound of money being inserted.
A number being dialled
followed by a ringing tone.

2

Mid shot of teenage girl with
receiver in hand.
worried expression on her face.

SOUND
Sound of phone being picked
up at other end. The girl
then speaks, hesitantly ....
" Brian ... hello Brian ...
is that you Brian ? ... "

3

SOUND

4

SOUND

Acknowledgements

The authors and publishers would like to thank the following for permission to reproduce copyright material:

BBC for Radio 4 Report on Nelson Mandela and Newsround Report on Nelson Mandela; Bloomsbury Publishing Ltd for extract from *Cat's Eye* by Margaret Atwood, Bloomsbury Publishing Ltd, 1989; John Carswell for *True Story* by Joan Ure; Faustin Charles for 'Legend' from *The Bluefoot Traveller*, ed. by James Berry, Nelson 1985; Collins for 'Hero' by Mick Gower from *Swings and Roundabouts; Daily Express* for report 'Drugs Killed Track Beauty' 27/11/87 and report 'Who says you can earn a mint out of begging? 12/12/89; David Higham Associates for 'Jigsaws' by Louis MacNeice and 'Road Up' by Norman Nicholson; *Early Times*, the National Weekly newspaper for young people, for Putting the Bullies on Trial, *Early Times* 11/1/89; Rosa Guy for 'She' from *Sixteen*; Barry Hines & Alan Stronach for extract from *Kes, the play*, Heinemann Educational 1976; *Kidscape* for 'Something to do if you are being bullied'; *Living Magazine* for *When Schooldays Turn into Nightmares*, 1990; Kara May for extract from *The End of the Road*; Methuen Children's Books for 'Mister Mushrooms' by Robert Swindells from *The Magnet Book of Sinister Stories*, Methuen 1983; *New Consumer* for 'Sharks in Raincoat' from New Consumer (pilot issue), May 1989; *National Canine Defence League* for extracts from their lealets which appear in 'A Dog is for life, not just for Christmas'; Judith Nicholls for 'What can you do with a pencil?' © Judith Nicholls 1987; Leslie Norris for 'A Tiger in the Zoo' from *Norris's Ark*, The Tidal Press, Maine, USA; Omni Publications International Ltd for 'I am large, I contain multitudes' from *The Best of Omni*, 1982; Oxford University Press for 'Truth' by Barrie Wade from *Conkers*, Oxford University Press 1989; Penguin Books Ltd for 'The Transport Cafe of her Nightmares' by Jan Mark from *Trouble Half Way*, Viking Kestrel 1985; Peters, Fraser & Dunlop for 'Back in the Playground Blues' by Adrian Mitchell from *I See A Voice*, Hutchinson 1982; Random Century Ltd for 'A Pottle o' Brains' from *The Woman in the Moon*, ed by James Riordan, Hutchinson 1984 and for extract from *Twopence to Cross the Mersy* by Helen Forrester, Bodley Head; Rogers, Coleridge & White for 'The Last Tiger' and 'The Fight' from *Salford Road and Other Poems* by Gareth Owen; Thames Television for extract from the television script of 'Rose' from Middle English; Virago Press for 'The Pig's Pudding' by Kathleen Dayus from *Her People*, Virago 1982.

Every effort has been made to contact copyright holders of material published in this book. We would be glad to hear from any unacknowledged sources at the first opportunity.

We would also like to thank the following for permission to reproduce photographs on the pages noted:

Allsport/Tony Duffy p 101; Birmingham Local Studies Centre pp 11, 13 14, 15; Camera Press pp 121, 122; Donald Cooper p 79 (bottom); Express Newspapers p 112; Rex Features 119 (top), 120; Fitzwilliam Museum, Cambridge, p 94; Format/R Kempadoo p 142 (bottom); Hutton Picture library, p 67; Liverpool City Council p 65; NHPA/Danegger p 142 (top); Chris Ridgers pp 17, 18, 19, 40, 41, 45, 50, 88, 89, 98, 115, 116, 117, 127, 134, 148; Royal Shakespeare Birthplace Trust pp 78, 79 (top), 85; Frank Spooner p 119 (bottom); Sally-Anne Thompson pp 104, 105, 110; Topham Picture Source p 64.